51 POWERFUL Ps of PUBLIC SPEAKING

ALSO PUBLISHED BY DAWN PUBLISHING

The Trilogy of Life Itself by Dawn Bates:
Friday Bridge – Becoming a Muslim,
Becoming Everyone's Business (2nd Edition, 2017)
Walaahi – A first-hand account of living through the Egyptian Uprising
and why I walked away from Islaam (2017)
Crossing The Line – A Journey of Purpose and Self-Belief (2017)
The Potent Power of Menopause: A Culturally Diverse Perspective of Feminine
Transformation by Dawn Bates and Clarissa Kristjansson (2022)

The Sacral Series by Dawn Bates:
Moana – One Woman's Journey Back to Self (2020)
Leila – A Life Renewed One Canvas at a Time (2020)
Pandora – Melting the Ice One Dive at a Time (2021)
Alpha – Saving Humanity One Vagina at a Time (2021)

The Democ-Chu Series by Nath Brye:
Slave Boy (2020)
BloodChild (2021)

Single titles:
Becoming Annie – The Biography of a Curious Woman by Dawn Bates (2020)
Becoming the Champion – V1 Awareness by Korey Carpenter (2020)
Unlocked by Carmelle Crinnion (2020)
Break Down to Wake Up by Jocelyn Bellows (2020)
Standing in Strength: Inspirational Stories of Power
Unleashed by Laarni Mulvey (2021)
The Recipe: A US Marine's Mindset to Success by Jake Cosme (2021)
Alive To Thrive: Life After Attempting Suicide –
Our Stories by Debbie Debonaire (2022)

51 POWERFUL Ps

of

PUBLIC SPEAKING

Impactful and Actionable Tips for
Any Speaking Engagement

by

KRYSTYLLE L. RICHARDSON

© 2022 Dawn Bates & Krystylle Richardson

Published by Dawn Publishing
www.dawnbates.com

The moral right of the authors has been asserted.

For quantity sales or media enquiries, please contact the publisher at the website address above.

Cataloguing-in-Publication entry is available from the British Library.

ISBN: 978-1-913973-30-8 (paperback)
       978-1-913973-32-2 (hardback)
       978-1-913973-31-5 (ebook)

Book cover design Miladinka Milic
Interior Layout Olivier Darbonville

All rights reserved. No part of this book may be reproduced, stored in a retrieval system, communicated or transmitted in any form or by means without written permission. All inquiries should be made to the publisher at the above address.

Disclaimer: The material in this publication is of the nature of general comment only and does not represent professional advice. It is not intended to provide specific guidance for particular circumstances and should not be relied on as the basis for any decision to take action or not to take action on any matters which it covers.

To discover more about Dawn Bates, the founder of Dawn Publishing, and the latest book releases, competitions and offers make sure you sign up for her regular weekly- ish emails using https://dawnbates.com/dive-in

Are you a writer? Do you want to get published? Then make sure you visit the home of Dawn Publishing at https://dawnbates.com/writers and see how Dawn can help you on your journey to becoming published!

Endorsements

In my twenty plus years of service as a soldier, and Military Intelligence Officer I have spent thousands of hours briefing senior leaders in the military. I have stood in front of hundreds of Soldiers and held their attention, delivered the commencement speech for dozens of graduations, and have spoken at so many promotions and reenlistments that I lost count. The Army has invested hundreds of thousands of dollars in my training to ensure I am able to quickly, concisely, and impactfully provide presentations and briefs that could save lives. Before reading Krystylle's book, I thought I knew all there was to know about executing powerful public speaking. I was excited to discover additional powerful techniques I hadn't yet explored. If you are ready to fall in love with being on stage and have the confidence and tools to deliver captivating presentations, this may very well be the only book you will ever need.

> **Jennifer James Mahoney - Major, Military Intelligence, U.S. Army, Founder, CEO, Author, Speaker**

As a public speaker, I would more than often speak from the heart and engage my audience when I felt the atmosphere was not conducive for receiving what I had to deliver. Once I became a professional speaker, one that speaks and presents for living, I realized to be impactful while speaking from the heart, I needed to prepare from the heart. The 51 Powerful Ps equips you to do just that. As a blueprint for the novice speaker or a checklist for those seasoned by their stage presence this work adds value across the board. You shall be empowered to empower others!

> **Darryl L. Rivers - Speaker, Trainer, Coach. Retired Hostage Negotiator, Owner of The Betterment Group**

This is truly a resource that should be in the hands of all public speakers on every continent. Over my many years in industry and as the founder of The Think and Grow Rich Institute, I have heard thousands of speakers live and online.

This book takes a practical approach and weaves in mindset, monetization and mastery of the speaking craft in a rather ingenious way. For those embarking on TedX Talks, stage presentations, speaking in a school setting or small groups this will truly be a valuable resource and a must have for all speakers worldwide. Congrats on a job well done.

> Satish Verma, President and CEO, Think and Grow Rich Institute

The simple and straightforward manner in which Krystylle presents what can seemingly be a daunting endeavor for most people, is brilliant. She provides context and stories that awaken the readers mind on how to deploy the strategies quickly and efficiently. this book is a must read for anyone seeking to share their message and make their mark in the world on stages of any size.

> Jen Du Plessis, The Impact Mentor, Kinetic Spark Consulting, LLC

If you desire to become an excellent communicator and connector of people, 51 Powerful Ps of Public Speaking is a must read. It will shape your mindset and provide you with step-by-step developmental skills to become an exceptional speaker.

> Rev Darryl Jackson, Sr. Pastor, New Home Baptist Church, Phoenix, AZ, Executive Director, LevelUp LLC, Certified Speaker & Coach, John C. Maxwell Corporation

This book is an amazingly thorough tool for new and even seasoned speakers! Krystylle covered every aspect of being a great speaker in such detail, and I really love the workbook element to it. This is the one book every speaker should read and apply the training to their careers!

> Carey Conley, Speaker, Author, Vision Expert & Coach

Krystylle Richardson nailed it in 51 Powerful Ps of Public Speaking! As a seasoned public speaker, I've studied the art of delivering a powerful presentation. This book is one of the best I've read that coveys the art of presentation delivery that can not only capture an audience but leave a lifelong impression that can change lives and shape cultures.

> **Travon Taylor, International Speaker, Best Selling Author**

I have been a speaker and a speaker coach for several years, and yet I have never sat down to consider how many Ps there were when it comes to public speaking. I am grateful that the author has done that for us. In this book, Krystylle Richardson displays a depth of knowledge and expertise, understanding and wisdom that clearly comes from her extensive background in public speaking. I personally know the author and I have seen her on stage in person, I have seen her on online summits and even on television. She is always consistent, authentic, heart-warming and connecting with her audience. Ms. Richardson's book provides not only theory and mindset training required to be an effective speaker, but also practical tools and challenges that the reader can, as she often writes in the book, "Wherever you are right now in the book, stop and…" she then outlines an exercise for the reader to put into Practice what they just learned.

With 51 different Ps to learn about, it is quite the challenge to choose favorites, however I like to highlight a couple. The author covers so many crucial aspects of being an effective public speaker such as 'Pitch and Patterns'. There are so many speakers today that seem to have either forgotten or have never been taught the importance of modulating one's voice tone, speed, volume, style and pattern or rhythm. Too many speakers think speaking is just opening one's mouth and saying words. It is not. The section on Polish stood out to me as well. It is not about perfection. But, as speakers, we should always be polishing our craft, our gift, so it can shine more brightly.

I also loved the section on non-Pity. Wow. The author explains that emotions may come when you speak. You may share a message that tugs on the heart of the audience, but the goal is never to invoke pity from the audience. Richardson states that impact is what we all should strive for as public speakers. And impact, I will say is the desired outcome for all who read **51 Powerful Ps of Public Speaking**. There is so much packed into these pages, and it absolutely should be one of the 'go to' books in your library on the topic of speaking.

Thank you, Ms. Richardson, for the work you do, how you serve and how you inspire, educate, and empower others to shine their light by sharing their voice. Well done.

> **Christoff J Weihman, International Speaker, Speaker Empowerment Coach, Creator & Producer of The Ultimate Speaker Competition, Co-Executive Producer of SPEAK UP on Amazon Prime Video/ Seasons 5 & 6**

51 Powerful Ps of Public Speaking, by Krystylle Lynne Richardson, is an outstanding book on the "how to's" of public speaking, including dealing with the anxiety associated with this endeavor. I found it to be inspiring in the sense it caused me to realize no matter how long one has been doing something, (in my case thirty-eight years), we never really arrive at 100% mastery. We should always seek new sources of knowledge, ideally, with the wisdom to properly apply this new information source. *51 Powerful Ps of Public Speaking* provides the reader with tools to excel in the crowded arena of public speaking.

51 Powerful Ps of Public Speaking can serve as a powerful effective resource for speakers on every level, as well as trainers and educators on how to develop into an effective public speaker.

If you are a public speaker, or, if you would like to start delivering effective engaging talks, this book is a must read.

> **James H. Carpenter Barnes, Ph.D. Best Selling Author & Public Speaker, Co-Founder of Life-Imagined LLC, Television and Podcast/ Radio Show Hosts, Co-Founder of The You Belong Foundation, Inc.**

Krystylle Richardson is an authority on what it is to command a stage. I have had the pleasure of working in the speaking industry with some of the most dynamic leaders. I've learned a lot about what it takes to engage and inspire an audience. If you are a speaker, this book packs more pattern, pitch, and power to ultimately create profit and a career accelerated by the prowess you harness from all the tips you receive from this book. A book with this much value makes it the easiest purchase decision of your life. I personally believe if a book like this could give you a speaking career, it should be priced at $10K. That is

ENDORSEMENTS

because I believe an author that reveals their secrets and wisdom should be compensated accordingly. Bottom line is Krystylle brings hope to those who believe their purpose is to speak and make a difference in the world. This book gives the methodology, strategy and tactics to take your game to the stage with 51 Powerful P's and Play BIG!

> Ken 'Dr. Smiley' Rochon, Jr., PhD, Author • Father • Speaker • World Traveller

51 Powerful Ps of Public Speaking by Krystylle Richardson is a groundbreaking and revelatory guide to effective public speaking in all arenas of life. Whether you are a seasoned professional or just embarking on your career, the *51 Powerful Ps of Public Speaking* will transform your public speaking career. From a platform of transparency, Krystylle walks you through her own process of learning about effective public speaking. She shares her personal trials and triumphs as a foundation for understanding not just the "how's" of good public speaking, but the "whys"—the basis for her selection of the 51 Powerful Ps. Each page of this extraordinarily successful work elegantly and eloquently also takes the reader through exercises to help apply the principles that will not only assist someone to overcome their fear of public speaking- but refine the craft of those who may have been speaking in front of small and large audiences for years.

I have taught trial advocacy for many years, and Krystylle's insight into the value of mimicking a tool to beginning one's public speaking journey is important in to establishing your own brand/identity as a public speaker. As an attorney, professor, pastor, CEO of my own company, and veteran public speaker, I have found the information in this phenomenal book invaluable.

The *51 Powerful Ps of Public Speaking* is a must read and sure to be a best seller! Thank you, Ambassador Krystylle, for sharing your experience, insight, and brilliance.

> Reverend Dr Sharon Anderson, Esq. Civility Ambassador, Attorney, Professor, CEO of KCG Consulting Services, LLC.

Foreword

If you are interested in becoming the best public speaker you can be, I urge you to read the *51 Powerful Ps of Public Speaking* by Krystylle Richardson.

This book will help you captivate your audiences and help you improve your overall presentation skills. This is not just another self-help book; it is a tool that can be used over and over again in order to master the art of public speaking.

I urge you to not only read, but also study and apply this book to your life.

Krystylle Richardson is an experienced speaker that has been all over the world and is sharing what she has learned, taught and applied with you.

I know you will gain a wealth of knowledge from this book, because I did, and I have been the CEO of the Napoleon Hill Foundation for twenty-one years.

Don Green
Executive Director
The Napoleon Hill Foundation
https://www.naphill.org

Dedication

This book is dedicated to all of those people who felt like there was no way they would ever be good at public speaking. It is also dedicated to those who have been too afraid to try, too afraid of failure, and who feel like those who do this well have some kind of magic powers.

The truth is, we all have the magic inside of us, it is called courage. Once we activate it, all things are possible, including the mastering of one of the biggest fears in the world, public speaking. So, here's to you.

Read this.

Apply it.

Go, speak, and let's change the world together with our powerful voices.

I dedicate this to you.

I dedicate this to us.

Gratitude

In dedication to my parents Theron and Verna Hodge. I would like to thank God for giving me my mind and my uniqueness.

I would like to thank my loving family Ben, Kelsey, Kayla, LeMont, Martha, Christopher, Mark, Vicki, Buddy, Eboni, and Mother-in-law Janice. Your support, love, encouragement, and smiles mean a lot.

To my elementary school teachers, Ms. Lupino, Mr. Schultz, and Mr. Walker at Ralph J Bunche School in Flint, Michigan, who had a tremendous impact on who I am today. To all of my teachers, pastors, mentors, and coaches in Flint, Detroit, Valparaiso, and Phoenix. I would also like to thank my cousin Kendall for her inspiration as a fellow author.

To my pastor Rev Davis, Dr HRH Rivers, Count and Countess John and Arlene Shin, my business partner Ron Klein, the late Frank Shankwitz, Ms. Lynda, Ms. Jackie, Ms. Donna, Ms. Julie, Pastor PD, Mr. Angel, Mr. Dezo, Ms. Laarni, my late cousin Michael, Brother and Sister James and Wendy, Mr Troy, Mr Josh, the women of WOIII, the Nex Gen Innovator delegates of Zambia and Ghana, The Forum, and all of the amazing people that continue to believe in me and pour into me.

Ms. Dawn, thank you for taking the time to be honest and therefore making me a better version of myself, and for helping me develop and add to the manuscript making this book the very best it could be.

Peace to all and remember to always believe in yourself. Always strive with all of your being for the ultimate success by positively re-creating the best you. In doing so, you will uplift those in need while cultivating the atmosphere of maximum impact.

To all those honored, mentioned, and quoted in this book — thank you so much.

Krystylle.

Contents

Publisher's Note	*xxi*
Who Should Read This Book?	*xxiii*
How to Use This Book?	*xxv*
Who Is Krystylle?	*xxvii*

POWER POSITION ONE: PREPARATION

1. Plan	3
2. Pretend	7
3. Prefer	10
4. Pronounce	14
5. Pitch and Patterns	16
6. Peek	19
7. Peter	21
8. non-Pity	23
9. Pie	24
Notes and Make Up Your Own Mind	27
Action Plan	28

POWER POSITION TWO: PERSPECTIVE

10. Positive	33
11 and 12. Pop and Pizzaz	36
13 and 14. Pupil and Pipes	38
15. Performance	40
16. Percent	42
Reflections	45
Notes and Make Up Your Own Mind	46
Action Plan	47

POWER POSITION THREE: POSE

17. Pose	53
Notes and Make Up Your Own Mind	62
Action Plan	63
Introducing	65

POWER POSITION FOUR: PRELUDE

18. Power	77
19. Point	80
20. Promise	84
21. Paid	87
22. Price	91
23. Partner	93
24. Polite	95
25. Plagiarism	97
26. Pile	99
27. Polish	101
Notes and Make Up Your Own Mind	104
Action Plan	105

POWER POSITION FIVE: PRIMETIME

28. Primetime Prep	111
29. Primetime Opener	115
30 and 31. Primetime Storytelling and Pirates	118
32. Primetime Points	120
33. Pure	122
34. Passion	124
35. Poking	128
36. Penetrate	130
37. Paint and Connect	132
Life Story Challenge – Try your hand at writing an engaging and inspiring life story	*135*

38. Pause	138
39. Pissed	141
40. Pick	143
41. Permanent	144
42. Ponder	146
43. Primetime Conclusion	148
44. Primetime Offer and Final Close	150
45. Protection	154
Notes and Make Up Your Own Mind	156
Action Plan	157

POWER POSITION SIX: POSTLUDE

46. Peace	163
47. Perfect	165
48. Plenty	168
49. Pudding	170
50. Please	172
51. Praise	174
Notes and Make Up Your Own Mind	177

About Krystylle Richardson	179
Additional Sheets for Future Use	182
Notes and Make Up Your Mind	183
Action Plan	184
Ephesians	186
About the Publisher	187

Publisher's Note

Speech is one of the key components in being able to bring about any kind of change in the world, whether this is pupils in the classroom, families at the dinner table, employees in the board room, or visionaries sharing from stages.

Without the ability to speak confidently, a purpose in mind, and without the need to read the "slides prepared earlier," many presentations may fall flat. They sometimes end up drier than the Sahara Desert and will soon lose the interest of the intended audience.

In today's world of "Lives" on social media and the ability to start and publish a podcast without the need for a studio and radio production teams of the past, the ability to speak in public has never been more important than it is now.

The events which unfolded in 2020 with the COVID health scare seem to have led to large amounts of gross misconduct of politicians, civil servants, and journalists and mass manipulation of information by the mainstream media. We also saw a huge increase in independent news channels popping up around the world, with news footage being shared by dark web platforms and highly encrypted messaging providers.

The good in this may be hidden in plain sight for some and may be very apparent for others. This increase in speaking outlets meant that more and more people were finding their voice, and, without realizing it, people were overcoming their fear of taking part in public speaking. Not all of the new participants in the realm of public speaking were good at it. For some, the passion led to great insight and amazing revelations plus interesting perspectives. For others, the passions and anger saw great messages lost in the lack of composure and structure of what to say, how to say it, and how to wrap up the message.

When Krystylle L. Richardson first came to me with this book, I had to consider whether it was on brand for my publishing company, especially as I focus on social change, human rights, social justice, and cultural diversity. Did this book fit my vision for my company? Did it align with all I stood for?

Absolutely it did! Because it is about giving people the confidence to own their voice, whilst giving a voice for those without a voice. It is also about guiding those with a voice to have a much more powerful voice in a world where it is becoming easier and easier for millions of people to share their message — even if many are getting lost in the crowd.

Working with Krystylle to develop the content, making it more culturally inclusive, deeper and richer has been eventful and challenging in a time when both inclusion and cancel culture negate one another.

The way in which this book has been designed means it works for everyone — regardless of the cultures within you and your audience, regardless of the platforms you intend to use to amplify your message, and regardless of the level of experience you have.

They say, "practice makes perfect," and yes it does when it is done with the intention of becoming better… but it also makes bad habits permanent. To have a guide such as this with you as you prepare for your live stream, podcasts, or news updates on your own news or YouTube channel, or on stage at a business event or political rally, will give you the power of credible confidence in front of audiences of 10 to 10,000,000.

Wishing the very best on your journey of amplifying your courage and your voice always,

Dawn
Writer, International Bestselling Author, Author Coach and Strategist, Publisher, Educator and Activist
https://dawnbates.com

Who Should Read This Book?

Anyone who is striving to be the best public speaker they can possibly be, regardless of where they are on their journey, will be my desired readers.

This book is a tool. Use it, grow, and use it again. Incorporate the techniques and tips in varying combinations until you find what fits and perfects YOU. Then, after that, go back through the book with your new level and new perspective and grow some more.

As you work to add to the freedom formula equation, let's dig deep into the seven pillars of power in public speaking. Even if you are already a dynamic public speaker, they can still be very helpful to you. The way I dissect the seven pillars of powerful public speaking is sure to spark a few creative things that you can try. I have done a lot of public speaking over the years. I've also had the honor and privilege to interview some of the giants and living legends of public speaking. I have interviewed some of the top motivators as well. I am delighted to share some of their secrets with you based on my study of their styles.

Speak with power. Live with power. Create a legacy.

Public speaking. Sometimes this is considered one of the, if not the, weirdest things that a person could try to do. Also, some people have what's called the gift of gab. Some people are very eloquent in what they say. Some people can captivate an audience in the first three seconds of being on stage. This can also relate to being in the boardroom or even speaking with your family. Some people have excellent communication skills in private, but it's a different thing when it's time to speak in public.

How to Use This Book?

There is no one method for using this book. Since it is a tool, it can be used as the reader decides what they need first. Here are some options that can be considered:

- Go from beginning to end.
- Go to the table of contents and see what you want to work on and go straight to those sections for some tips.
- Use it how you would like, just use it, come back to it often, share it, and grow from it. Partner with someone or a group, pick a powerful P and work together to master it, then move on to another.
- Read a few of the powerful P's and write some of them on a paper and put them in a basket. Pull out a paper and see what is on the paper. Attempt to use the skill for that powerful P and master it. Make a game out of it, and have people score you or discuss how you did. Have fun with it as you build your skill.

You can grab the full and complete workbook
to accompany this book by visiting
https://krystyllerichardson.com/51Psworkbook

Who Is Krystylle?

My name is Krystylle Richardson, and when I look back to my childhood, I remember doing speeches when I was a child in school as well as in church. During my school years, I remember looking around to see people's facial expressions to find out whether I was doing well or not. It's funny how those memories then stemmed over into adulthood and the career paths we take in life. Some of the speeches I delivered in churches were when I was a child, through my youth, bringing me to present day. The churches in Michigan, Indiana, and Arizona were where I grew in confidence as a speaker, and Arizona is where I have chosen to make my hometown. Some of the topics I chose had to do with understanding our purpose, how to be a servant leader, communicating with various levels of leadership, as well as how to perform various types of services based on the occasion, dance or choir workshops to name a few.

Some of my speeches as a child at Ralph J Bunche in Flint, Michigan, were science based such as understanding how tendons worked. When I was a child, I would go hunting with my dad, and if we shot a duck or a goose, I would take the foot into school and do "show and tell." I would demonstrate the tendons' function and motion by moving the feet. I had an interesting childhood, and the teachers loved my presentations. So did the geeky and gross boys, the girls, not so much. After all, my speech was not of the normal flowery and delicate nature as was the norm back then; it was about a dead bird's foot. They were good times, and I love reminiscing about those speeches.

Over the years, I have done a lot of public speaking, some of which have gone well, and some have not. I've spoken all over the world, and whilst I have lost count of the number, it's probably about thirty countries or so, and that is LIVE and in person, with countless others in the online space. I've spoken on four continents, which is increasing due to the number of virtual live events. The live events have been in Jamaica, Bahamas, and Barbados, regarding dance, medical, and ministry missions. My husband and I have also joined forces to teach vacation bible school, which goes over scriptures, arts and crafts, and sermon items. Speaking in Ghana, Nigeria, and Senegal for missions and medical projects was a joy and was in conjunction with taking equipment collected from companies in the United States, which we would barter in exchange for medication to treat the orphan children in need. I led most of the trips and did most of the speaking, preaching, and bartering. With medical and ministry missions in Kenya, along with missions and medical trips, which have taken me all over Europe and Asia speaking and doing training for genetic research and medical device companies, I have gained a huge amount of experience in cultural communication and understanding.

Some of my materials had to be translated into Mandarin so the students could read both the English and Mandarin versions whilst I spoke. In those cases, I had to speak slower and with more intent. There was an interpreter, plus the English and Mandarin paper copy. This was a great experience and humbled me as a speaker. I could not "Go! Go! Go!" as Americans do. I had to slow down and rephrase for conciseness and clarity vs loud, roaring verboseness.

One thing is true about them all, sometimes they were easy, sometimes not so easy, and sometimes I'm full of confidence, sometimes not so much. Regardless of whether I find it hard or easy, filled with confidence or dread, I just keep going. I keep giving my all. I do what I have to do.

I have a very deep faith and believe God has specifically placed me on this Earth to be a blessing to others in many ways. I do that through what I call life innovation. I remember several moments that woke me up to this fact. Once was when I turned into oncoming traffic after falling asleep at the wheel while driving, the lane, which was normally very busy, was empty, but it did not stop my heart from pounding hard. I thanked God for his grace and vowed to do his will.

Another time was when the doctors discovered a tumor on my left kidney. I went to the hospital for a pain in my right side and they found a tumor of the left. I again vowed to serve and help as many as I could in their businesses and spiritually.

There are lots of these stories that I will share, a few more here and some in other written works. The point is that none of us are one-dimensional beings. We all have been through things in various areas of life. We all live by eating, so we need the health innovation portion of life innovation. We also need to make money by doing something purposefully, unleashing the innovation portion of our life. We all have some type of connection with a higher power, so we need WOKE the kingdom innovation portion of life innovation. The elements of life innovation are to be surrounded by a circle of influence that helps us to be total well-rounded individuals, creating impact daily.

The things I share when I speak and when I write have to do with various aspects of life. Sometimes I am talking to elementary school students that are packed 400 strong in school assemblies. The topics range from big dreams in action to motivation regarding career choices, leadership, and even drum and dance as demonstrated for all continents.

Other times, I am on stage or even in a board meeting with only two people. No matter the instance, I must ensure that I have included the right combination of the powerful pieces included in this book. Without the right combination, I may not have the impact that I had hoped. I have a strong desire to serve humanity, a strong desire to positively affect the state of civility in the world. I am highly driven and attract individuals who want to do the same in their own lives. Is that you? Is that why you are reading this book?

A lot of people have a fear of public speaking; that's why it's even higher on the ranking of fears than even death. At first that seemed surprising to me, until I was afraid, and then I realized I didn't want people to have to go through some of what I did on my journey in public speaking. Having some barriers that held me back made fear bigger than my thought of success. Fear is a big driver to take people down a road of I cannot vs the road of I can. I recently went skydiving for the first time and conquered that fear. As I continue to do things like that, I get stronger and stronger as a person and as a speaker. Emotions are known to be transferrable. Lack of confidence in one area transfers to other areas in our life. Speaking is affected by our life, not just our words.

This book is meant to be an aid, a guide, something that you can use for the rest of your life to build you up, to give you hope, and to hone your skills. We all go up and down in all of these from time to time. Public speaking is something that happens while you're still alive and you can feel the after effect of it as you go through each day praising yourself because you did well or beating yourself up because you don't think that you did well. Death on the other hand, when it's over it's over, right? Exactly. So having the fear of public speaking be the highest fear that people have then becomes understandable.

After having COVID months back, my breathing changed and now my lung capacity is different. I even feel that my vocal cords have gone through a change. With all of that being said, sometimes my words don't come out as strong as I would have hoped. Utilizing some of the techniques in this book has helped me to overcome these new challenges, and in the times that I don't overcome it, I just talk about it. I realize that if you face your fears and bring them out to the open and let people know that there's an issue or fear, then it's easier for you to get past it. Leaving it inside of you only builds up stress and can cause you to run off the virtual or physical stage in fear and in a ball of embarrassment.

I've had that thought many times, but I stayed the course. Some would say I am stubborn; others would say dedicated.

Being a big numbers person, I need a measure, so having a list of powerful elements, regardless of which area of life we are wanting to improve, makes sense to me. I have felt for a while that in the arena of public speaking we needed something to measure ourselves against, something that is a great gift to the world. I believe statistics guides us on where we were and where we might want to go next. Numbers help guide our talks, speeches, and lectures because they create a foundation for our "Why." Coming up with a way to measure how well we're doing in public speaking falls right into that. I was excited when I came up with the index and hope that the people that read this and utilize it are too.

I used some of these Powerful Ps during my recent EMERGE experience, a media mastery event that I regularly hold as a live event. The delegates did a great job utilizing a number of the tools in this book. My hope is that this book is something that new speakers and seasoned speakers can use to help them, as it has helped me, well into the future.

During the course of this book, I will be taking you through a series of scoring lessons. You will not see the scoring at the end of Power Positions 1, 2, and 3 until after section 3. This is because I would like for you to get a feel for how the positions work first, gain value from them, then move into scoring. Putting the scoring at the end of the first chapters would detract you from digging into the methodologies in my view. So, keep reading and know that the score will start at position 3 and continue then at the end of each position through to the end of the position description.

None of us know what the future will hold, but what I can say is that this book has helped me get some of my thoughts on paper, things that I've been doing to help myself and others for many years. I hope this helps you to understand a little bit more about why I did what I did in this book. I wish the best to everyone. I'd also love to hear your stories on how you've conquered each Powerful P that is in this book. Please share.

I wrote this book to help you to learn from my truths. I wrote it to share so you can be a stronger and more impactful speaker. I go into some of the things that I have learnt and discovered over the years, the things which could be considered my strengths, as well as the things I needed to work on. I would venture to say that no speaker is 100% on all 51 of the items in this book. I know that I'm not. This is something I still use today as a checklist for me of whether I'm projecting, or if I am the Peter, as well as where am I presenting and speaking with power.

When we're speaking in any way, we want to know the people are resonating with what it is that we're saying. I still have that feeling of being a little girl looking around to see if people are agreeing or disagreeing or even paying attention to what I'm saying. All too often we rely on other people for validation, so this book has been written to give you a way of evaluating yourself with the measuring methods that are included. It is a book which has been in me for many, many years, so I'm thrilled to be able to get it out into the atmosphere finally and into your hands, your mind, and especially your soul. I have put off this book because of life happening day after day. This book, like others, had become something that I came across on my to do list, or in my document searches. I would say to myself, I must make more time to get this book done. After years of this cycle happening, I was at a point in my life where I saw a great need to help people in media mastery. This was specifically in the area of public speaking, developing their own speaker style, mastering their content structure and many other components. I would have people come up to me after my talks and say how it inspired them, how great of a speaker I was and a number of other nice words. Some said that after they heard me talk, it did not matter whether I was selling a program or not, they wanted in on whatever I was doing next. It was then that I knew that I needed to not make time but create time to get this book out. Since then, I have used bits and pieces of the philosophies in this book to help my clients and am happy that the collection of some of my speaking journey is captured here to help even more.

I hope and I pray this book positively impacts your life, your dreams, and your destiny. I also hope that any newly found skills and progress will also increase your finances and influence and make you an audience favorite. All of the notes above are important to me, for you, because it helps me to know that I have fulfilled a portion of my purpose for being on this Earth. One of my main desires is to help people be the best versions of themselves. Powerful public speaking can help you do that, and share your best self with the world, over and over again.

With love, gratitude, and blessings always,
Krystylle.

Colossians 4:6 – Let your speech be always with grace, seasoned with salt, that ye may know how ye ought to answer every man.

Bible KJV

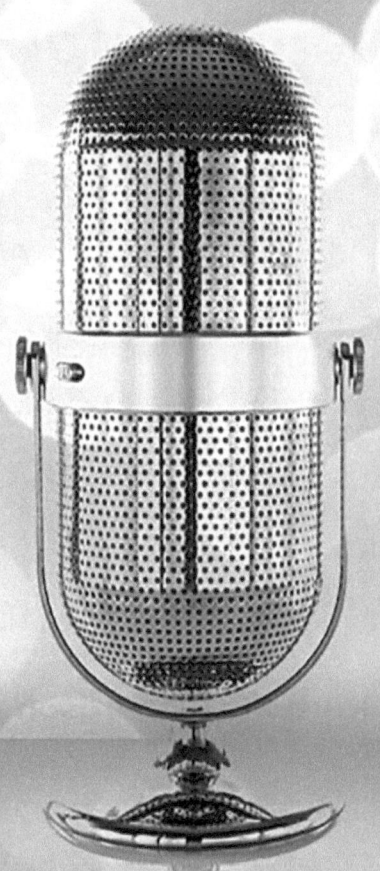

"Being powerful takes preparation. Set your mind to the intention. Prepare to be powerful. The person with the floor, with the mic, with the attention, has the power to shift the atmosphere. Prepare to be a shifter, in the right direction. Prepare for takeoff. Prepare for positive impact."

Krystylle Richardson

1

Plan

How awesome it is when a plan comes to life. Plans for our business, our next meal, our vacation, our wedding, our route to get to our big interview, or our financial plans for our next interesting investment or even for retirement, if there is such a thing. Plans are important and sometimes can make or break our successful outcome. So, my question for you is, are you a planner? Do you see the value of having a detailed plan that you execute? Are you the type of person that just sketches a few points on a napkin and then goes for it? Do you write a plan and bounce it off of friends and family? All of the above are fine depending on the importance of the plan. Let's dig a little further.

I love teaching on focusing and planning. Plans, however, do not mean anything if we lack energy in action related to execution. Planning requires us to first have an imagination and a thought of what it is we want to do.

Before we talk about public speaking, I want to first have our minds focus on the word "plan" and how we use it in everyday life.

1) Take for example our existence. Our parents may have planned to have a child or may not have, yet we are here.

2) Example two: You may have planned to go to the store to get three items, yet you walk out of the store having purchased five times as many items than you had planned.

3) Last example: A gentleman may have a plan in his head of how he is going to propose to the lady he adores. When it comes time for

the actual proposal, the spot for the proposal is wet because it has been raining for two days, the store for the flowers he wanted to have closed early due to a family emergency, the street has a closure sign on it due to a problem with a tree being down. The gentleman could be discouraged by portions of his plan being turned upside down. He could also think about how he could make the best of his original plan and add on changes to still make their day special.

The same goes for public speaking. We may have a plan to talk about three main points, and by the time we see the audience, feel the energy of the audience, experience the venue, overcome a microphone glitch or two, our plan may have shifted to different points, or may have stayed the course. So, are plans in general important? The answer is yes. Are plans a good idea in public speaking? The answer is still yes. A big aspect of planning is having a creative mind and a mind that can wrap its energy around the possibility of change.

In the technical world that I spend time in regularly, there is a technique called six sigma. Some of the various tools and techniques related to six sigma had been developed and implemented by Japanese businesses, and I still use it today as a model for continuous improvement. One of the biggest areas focused on is related to the definition of a problem and the resulting plans. A lot can be learned from this technique, but I will not go into that in the Powerful Ps of public speaking other than to say that a good amount of time should be spent in planning. Part of planning is understanding who your audience is and tailoring your talk for that purpose.

This is an interesting quote:

God is, even though the whole world deny him. Truth stands, even if there be no public support. It is self-sustained.

Mahatma Gandhi

Plan to have truth in your talks. Be ok with people agreeing with you and not agreeing.

Another part of planning is not just your audience, but also the venue. Based on the venue and if there are microphones that are handheld or lapel mic, or a podium or no podium, all of this goes into how you will plan to deliver your message. Some people use PowerPoint or audio and visual methods. Whatever your preference is related to these methods, you should have a plan for using all the items mentioned, and you should also have a plan if some of those items do not work. For instance, if the microphone goes out, is there another microphone that can be used? If there is not another microphone that can be used, does your voice project loud enough for you to get your message out to the crowd? If it is a larger venue and everyone is spread out, are you able to have everyone come closer to you and gather at the front of the auditorium to be able to hear you better for you to get your message to them? If everyone is seated, can you walk around and give portions of your message to various portions of the venue? This is just one example of a microphone going out.

All these things that I have mentioned above are things that I've seen happen. And some techniques that I've had to use myself. The point is if the message was important enough for you to write it and for you to accept the speaking engagement, then you should do whatever you need to do to make sure that you deliver that message. So, plan for the best and plan for hiccups. Do not let the hiccups stress you out. Use your strength and keep going until you get the job done. Of course, there is something called the point of no return. This is where you've tried two, three, or even five things, and it keeps getting worse and worse, and you may not be able to get your message out. At that point, you can even let everyone know that you will record it and send it to them.

Another thing you can do to help plan as part of being a powerful public speaker is to have a team. This may be a team of one, but it is still a team.

What do I mean by this?

Being a public speaker of any kind means that you need to concentrate on what it is that you plan to say, in my opinion. Having someone there to help take care of tech support issues with the audio-visual team or even fix that strand of hair that is out of place is a big help. Of course, you can do all of this yourself. The point is you don't have to be Superman or Superwoman. Some people have a paid assistant or a person that travels with them. Other people have a family member go along. Whatever your scenario, do yourself a favor and accept the help. A lot of venues, as well as conferences, have people specifically assigned to each speaker to assist with these kinds of needs. That is not the case in every situation. My main point here is to use the staff or use the help because it will allow you to focus on what you are about to say. Even if you've done that particular talk a million times, it's still some help to have planned support. Suppose this is not something that you can line up before your speaking engagements, no worries. The main thing is to never give up, even if technical issues come up. Work through it with the team, keep a level head, and do your thing.

Do not be defeated.

Plan, plan again, and plan some more. You will thank yourself for following these three steps. What three steps? Plan, plan again, and plan some more.

2

Pretend

Let's jump into a little interaction for this one, shall we. Take a moment to focus yourself and maybe have five or even twenty minutes to dedicate to this little exercise.

Did you block out a small amount of time?

Are you ready to begin?

Yes? Ok. Go to the mirror. Pick a speaker you look up to. If you do not have a favorite speaker yet, then, just listen to a few speakers on YouTube before this exercise and pick one that you like. This will be the person you will use to answer the questions in this section. This is just for fun, so there are no worries if you are not madly in love with the person you chose.

Exercise: Think about what they would do. Think about what they would say. Let's start with their opener. How do they open? Pretend to be them for a moment. Next, what do they do? Do they tell stories? Do you remember one? Tell a portion of a story you remember from them. Next, did they take you on a journey? Act like you are taking your audience on their journey. Just pretend with me for a moment. Next, let's just jump to the closing. How do they close? Mimic their close as well.

Now, how did all this feel? Did you feel weird or uncomfortable? That might be the case, but did it make you think about their style? The point of this exercise was style and delivery. What did you like about their style AFTER doing the pretend exercise? Write down seven things you liked and seven things you did not like. What did you like about the energy and delivery, use of the stage (in your case a mirror), use of hand gestures, etc.? Write down five things you liked and did not like.

Pretending and mimicking sometimes gives you an insight that you would not have from just listening to a person. It is the DO part of learning that helps us sometimes more than simply passive learning styles.

Based on this short exercise, figure out what types of techniques that you just demonstrated that you want to include in your style and delivery. Do not do all of them one-for-one. Be yourself, just use some hints from your list of greats. If you have developed a style without this, then that is terrific. If not, then this sometimes helps to gain some tangible hints as to what you want to have as your foundational powerful public speaking style.

Go for it. I cannot wait to see you do your thing. Contact me to share a video of you speaking if this tip was helpful. Another thought is to write down your favorite scriptures regarding pretending and pretense. Do you have any?

Love this scripture regarding "Pretend."

We can pretend and we can also be taught what to say: Exodus 4:12 - Now therefore go, and I will be with thy mouth, and teach thee what thou shalt say.

3

Prefer

A few questions:
- When it is time for a carbohydrate of some sort, do you pick a donut or a bagel?
- When you go on vacation, do you decide to go to the mountains, the beach, the cabin in the woods, to the big city, or on the boat?
- When it is time to acquire a company, do you prefer start-ups or mature companies
- When you moved out on your own, did you immediately go out and buy a pet or decide on no pets?

The answers to these questions are linked to the word that is the focus on this section. We will also do some pretending. As we pretend and practice and pretend some more, we will learn our own style. This brings us to the word "Prefer." It is my hope that you do not get stuck in preferences, however. Sometimes this word causes speakers to grow stagnant. You will read time and time again in this book that you must know your audience. This means that when speaking you do not always go for what you know, you go for what the audience needs. How do you know what that is? Easy. Talk to them. Go early to the venue, chat with some on social media, go to the restroom and talk in there (great stuff happens in the women's restroom, guys, so sorry you cannot experience this). Go to lunch with some of the audience. Invite some to sit at your table. Stand at the door of the conference area and welcome some of them to the event even if it is not your event. Let them know you will be speaking. Ask them their name, hometown, and ask them a survey-type question regarding your talk. Remember where they are sitting and refer to them during your talk. This then allows you to mix what you prefer to talk about with new content learned from the audience you are about to serve. This is one of the biggest tips of the trade that I see successful speakers do consistently. It works. It also can get you more sales of your books and course at the end of your talk. This Powerful P is priceless.

"Do not be so self-involved when you are about to speak that you forget to learn more about who you are speaking to. This is truly priceless."

Krystylle Richardson

- Step 1: At your next in-person event, use this method.
- Step 2: Welcome three people to the event even if it is not your event — get their names and two facts about them.
- Step 3: Talk to three more people during lunch — get their names and two facts about them.
- Step 4: Mention them in your talk and at least one of the facts — work it into your talk.
- Step 5: Thank them later for coming — ask them if there was something that they resonated with in your talk — ask if there is something they would prefer to hear more about in the future.
- Step 6: Perfect your craft as the world's next most powerful public speaker.
- Step 7: Celebrate your wins and your encouragement of yourself to be better.

You can grab the full and complete workbook to accompany this book by visiting
https://krystyllerichardson.com/51Psworkbook

4

Pronounce

How do you say what you say? Do you use high pitches, or low? Do you check the proper way to say a word that you don't know, before you say it, or do you simply give it a go? Do you get confused when someone is speaking, and that one word comes out in a manner that you have never heard before? If that happens, does it throw off the whole mood of their presentation because you are still fixated on that one word? This has happened to me while attempting to listen to a speaker, and it took me a while to bounce back.

The fact is pronunciation is so important. Public speaking takes us into the classroom at this point. The classroom could be at your own home when you are preparing for your speech. Make sure that you understand every word that you plan to say. Make sure you know the meaning of it and the correct pronunciation. There's nothing worse sometimes than a speaker who did not do their homework and did not know how to pronounce words that they've written in their speech. I've heard this in small groups and large auditoriums. I've heard this in sermons as well as in virtual summits. Please, please do your homework and have all your words ready to roll off of your tongue with ease.

Another thing I want to say about pronunciation has to do with speed and character. You could rock your talk by pronouncing a word very slowly with elegance, fast with brawn, swanky, or soulful. This adds color and flavor to your talk. Use this power wisely. Also, don't use it too often. If every five minutes you're doing this, it could be that you added into maybe the comedy portion of what you're doing. But consider this a special power that is just used to add a little bit of spice. Now that you have this tip, it is up to you and how you use it.

This is not a long section in this book but is a very important one. The last thing I will say is related to owning it. If something comes up that is a word that you do not know, own it. You can build that into your talk. You can easily say I'm not sure how to say this word, but I'm going to give it a go. Or you could say does anyone know how to say this word, and then you could spell it. You can turn it into an audience participation moment. There are various ways to get beyond something like that. One other way is if you mess it up, you can say oh my gosh I just really messed that up, who knows how to pronounce this word. you could then give them a free book or a gift card or have the audience give them a round of applause. Owning it is a great tool to use in a lot of situations. I have to own things all the time. It builds character.

5

Pitch and Patterns

How about we mix it up a bit?
Based on the event and audience, this section can be lots of fun. Time to go up, go down, weave in tones, pitches, and patterns to create a masterpiece of symphonic melody during your talk. Yes, you read it correctly. Symphonic melody. Your talk can truly take on a world of its own, creating a masterful picture for the listeners that leaves them feeling like they were in a speech art gallery. After all, a beautiful portrait, a delightful landscape, and a simple photo of a rose can all bring about a strong emotion of wow. The same can happen in a masterful speech. This is why we are now going to discuss pitch and patterns. This is one of the fun areas of public speaking. Getting into your speech is something that can help people get something out of your speech. Let me say that again in a different way. Your excitement breeds excitement. Using your voice is a key part of that. If you have a deep voice normally, using a few mid-tones or higher tones during your talk will give it flavor. If you have a high voice, the opposite is true. Force yourself to use some lower tones—variety spices up your talk. You've heard the word monotone. Do you want to be classified as a monotone speaker? I think not. You have greatness inside of you. Everyone does. Part of the reason that you're reading this book is to help get your greatness out to the world. So why not use your voice to spice it up a bit.

Some people, as I have mentioned in other sections of this book, use the formula of "say what you're going to say, say it, and say what you said."

Pitch and Patterns

You can use various methods to do this. Part of it has to do with the speed of your voice. Saying words quickly to get the point across is fine. Having it be that the whole speech is fast might be an issue—the same as if it is slow. Talking too slow does not necessarily keep the attention of the audience. It does help, however, if you're saying something that's very complex for you to say it more gradually. I also use repetition during these times. I've seen this time and time again with a number of the successful public speakers that I work with daily. So don't be afraid to slow it down. Also, don't be afraid to speed it up. The worst thing is to keep everything mid-speed and bore your audience. You can tell this based on another section that I have in this book related to looking out to see how engaged people are and what it is that you're talking about.

A good pattern to have in your voice emphasizes what you're saying, especially during storytelling. Some people use various voices during storytelling. What I mean by this is if a man is speaking and he's telling something that a woman said, then he may use a feminine voice pattern. The same for a female if she wants to explain that a man said something or even that they heard the voice of God, they might use a deeper tone. Hopefully, you're getting the point here that variety with your tone, pitch, and even modulation will help the audience get a clear picture of what you're trying to convey. They may even come up to you afterward and say, wow, that story was so interesting. You made the characters come alive. I really enjoyed how you told that story. I felt like I was in a movie. Various things have been said to me as well as other people that do public speaking which lets you know that you did it. You used your pitch in voice patterns to make your topic come alive. This is sometimes something that takes practice, so don't beat yourself up if you are not there yet. Again, this is why you are reading this book.

Picking up various tools and tricks and techniques is what it's all about. As you go through all of the Powerful Ps, pick out ones that are most important for you based on the topic that you are going to speak on. You may need to work one set of the power positions for the talk you have this week. Next week you may need to look through the book and work on another set of power positions; whatever you do, continue to use this book as a resource to help you grow and thrive as a public speaker. The people that have been on my shows and that are in my circle make hundreds and thousands of dollars speaking. That can also be you. Hopefully, you take this as a challenge. It would be great to hear from you when you get the first speaking engagement that you get paid for. Also, would be great to hear from you once you get your asking price based on being a keynote speaker. This comes with time, and it also comes because of implementing all of the power positions such as those outlined in this book.

6

Peek

Can you feel your heartbeat going faster?
It is time to get your audience engaged and excited. It is time for anticipation. How do you feel when you know that something great is coming? Whether it be a newborn baby's birth, or a delicious meal that you know is about to be delivered to your table, or a new song that is being released by your favorite artist in the next week or two. You say to yourself: What is coming? What is next? What does the audience have to look forward too? How excited are you about what you are currently saying and about what is coming next?

Great questions, I am so glad that you asked! Just kidding. But seriously, this is a big deal in public speaking. Keeping your audience engaged, keeping them on the edge of their seat, so to speak, is a big part of what makes great speakers great. Having great connectivity from one segment of your talk to the other is great for you to keep up with what you are saying next and for the audience to keep them engaged. I just might say engaged or engagement a few more times in this section because it is so important. After all, a memorable speaker is one that not only has something important or impactful to say, but one that knows how to say it. Have you ever heard a speaker who has a very similar message as someone else, but their delivery didn't grab you, did not call you to action, did not make you want to jump to your feet and yell "heck yeah!!!!!" Well, why is that? My answer: engagement and connection. Energetically use the sneak peek method discussed in this section and see your engagement go up. I love to enact the sneak peek. I get excited about what is next. I hope you can try it and see how it works for you.

7

Peter

There once was a swimmer who wanted to be the best in his region. The problem was that he had an endurance issue. He was able to make it about two or three laps in the pool, but to qualify for the regionals, he needed to be able to do five. He practiced and practiced every day for at least three hours per day. Even with doing breaks and getting back in the pool he was not able to make it to five laps in time for the try outs. He was however able to make it to four laps. The last bit needed to go to five laps though, seemed like a goal that could never be reached. He would just "peter out" each time. He would lose his breath and would have to get out every time. For this reason, some of the mean children, would call him Peter.

Poor Peter. Why do I say? Because this has to do with a person petering out during their talk. What I mean by that is they had a great opening; they talked about what points they were going to talk about. They also may have even had great engagement with the audience. But then something happened. They lost their energy. They lost their thought process. They lost their purpose. When you understand the purpose for why you are doing what you're doing, it makes it easier to keep the fire. When you have practiced and know what you're going to say, it is easy to keep your fire and not peter out. If you have done all of the preparation, if you have powered up your mindset by using the acronym PUSH, power up to stay high, you will not peter out. If you feel this happening, you need to have enough discernment about your own speaking skills to shut that down immediately. You can also tell that based on the audience. But if you're doing this based on an online summit, you may or may not know what the audience reaction is if you cannot see comments. So, you have to power up yourself, you have to stay high yourself, and make sure you do not peter out yourself.

So, let's do the best we can to get a good night's sleep. Let's do the best we can to have great preparation. Have whatever meal plan or vitamins or supplements that you need to be ready with preparing the inside of your body so that you don't peter out on the outside. Let's keep those great facial expressions and use those hand gestures and all of the things that you have been trying to do to come out with power and end with power. Do not invoke the spirit of Peter during any of your talks.

If you feel that coming on, go and find my definition of push and let's do this. Let us also send positive energy to our little swimmer Peter. Maybe, just maybe, with the effects of our positive energy, Peter can now make it to the end of the fifth lap, so he can qualify for the swim race.

Here's to you Peter. The next race has your name on it.

&

Here's to you, the worlds next post powerful speaker.

8

non-Pity

Homeless. Let us use our compassion to give our brothers and sisters a hand up and not just a handout. This is an active and actionable response. Most of the people that we serve as part of our non-profit just need a little help to get back up on their feet. So, active and actionable compassion is way better than just a handout. This can also be said for a public speaker. Let us now shift this concept over to public speaking, we want them to feel our talk. Taking your audience to a place of compassion is good. Taking them to a place of having pity is not good. This is not the emotion that we should be trying to invoke when doing any kind of speaking engagement. This Powerful P is here so we intentionally review our speeches and ensure that the emotion radar is on. No pity, just compassion and strength. If your audience can see that you used a vulnerable moment in your life and gained strength from it, this is a good thing. They can then have compassion while also witnessing your strength.

9

Pie

Ok dessert lovers, this section is for you. Well, maybe not as a dessert, but the concept of pie makes me think of dessert. Yum. Speech writing can be easy and fun and sometimes can be hard work depending on your perspective. My hope for you is that you do not beat yourself up for not having the speech be exactly as you had hoped. Powerful speakers go with the flow of the moment as well as with preparation. I called this section pie. This means I am going to take what I have and make the most of it. I like pie. Peach pie especially. No matter how the writing turns out, I will deliver pie to my audience. Most people like pie. My hope is that you are one of them, and that you love mine.

You see, lots of people make pie. Even when using the same recipe, the pie is bound to come out slightly different. This is the same for public speaking in every case. What I mean is, that even if there are two pastors that use the same scripture to preach from for instance, the sermons will be totally different. The same for motivational speakers. Say there are five people (I love to do this in my speaker camps). They all have the same subject. There may be some overlap, but I can absolutely guarantee that the speeches will be different. Why is that?

Guess 1: _____
_____
_____
_____
_____

Guess 2: _____
_____
_____
_____
_____

Guess 3: _____
_____
_____
_____
_____

Part of the reason the speeches will be different is because we have all been created different. We come from different places. We have had different experiences. We have some same and differing religious beliefs, food preferences, and more. This list could go on and on, but the point is that this is what would make our talks different. Not just different but each uniquely intriguing. I simply love this about public speaking, don't you?

You can grab the full and complete workbook to accompany this book by visiting https://krystllerichardson.com/51Psworkbook

> "Pie is delicious. Make your public speaking invoke the same type of delight that pie does. You will have a winning career in speaking for sure."
>
> **Krystylle Richardson**

NOTES and MAKE UP YOUR OWN MIND

ACTION PLAN

Issue: _____

_____

_____

_____

Why should I work on this? _____

_____

_____

_____

What is my desired outcome? _____

_____

_____

_____

_____

Steps to work on this – list top 3 to 5 steps: _____

_____

_____

_____

_____

_____

This must be done by (timeframe/date): _____

_____

_____

If this does not happen, what is the negative effect: _____

_____

_____

_____

_____

I proclaim that I will: _____

_____

_____

_____

_____

_____

_____

_____

_____

_____

_____

Stop where you are in this book. Time to practice.
Pick 3 of the Powerful Public Speaking Ps
Write what it is about these 3 that you want to perfect
Practice 7 times over a set period of time
Each time, take notes and adjust as needed
Determine your score or have others determine a score
Are you getting better each time?

Powerful Public Speaking P Date: Practice # :	Score (1-10)	
1.		
2.		
3.		

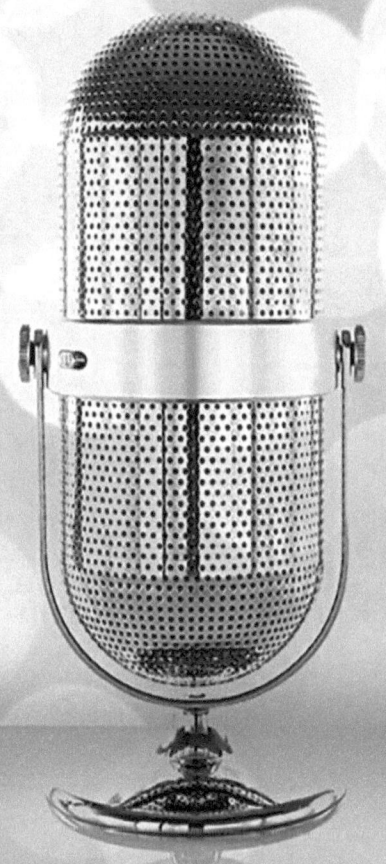

Power POSITION 2

PERSPECTIVE

"Until we look at our public speaking as the soul-tapping tool that it is, we may never truly be powerful. Public speaking is a way to tap into the listeners destiny, legacy, and God-given purpose. Use this power wisely."

Krystylle Richardson

10

Positive

There is nothing that beats positivity.
There is nothing that beats light, upbeat, and shine.
There is nothing that beats the ability to ooze good vibes. Yes, I said ooze.

The light and power that dwells in you should be able to be seen from miles around. Especially on stage. After all, who does not like a positive speaker? There are some, I am sure. The point is that the stage, whether LIVE or virtual, is your time to do your do. Some of the most powerful speakers have their own way of demonstrating positivity. Here is a list of some of the positive ways and mannerisms of the powerful. See if you recognize any of them in your favorite speakers and in yourself.

During my travels, I have noticed a number of cultural norms that I would like to highlight here regarding positivity and public speaking. The list below is things to think about based on the country you may be in and is not meant to be an exact rule to follow.

Positivity listing (Caution: Use based on discernment and with caution. All of these notes in the section do not fit every speaking scenario. Some of these have been used by some of the most influential speakers of our time. Just because they work for them, does not mean they will work for you. This is meant to be a general guide only. I suggest that you do your own research, ask questions to your event producers and make your own judgements as to what to do.

America	Europe	Asia	Africa
Smile	Smile	Smile	Smile
Know what is trending economically and touch on it if it fits.	Know what is trending economically and touch on it if it fits.	Know what is trending economically and touch on it if it fits.	Know what is trending economically and touch on it if it fits.
Have a good intro, hook to lead them from section to section of your talk and a call to action at the end.	Have a good intro, hook to lead them from section to section of your talk and a call to action at the end.	Have a good intro, hook to lead them from section to section of your talk and a call to action at the end.	Have a good intro, hook to lead them from section to section of your talk and a call to action at the end.
Pop and be energetic. Use hand gestures that are specific to that culture	Use hand gestures that are specific to that culture (take caution to not offend)	Use hand gestures that are specific to that culture (take caution to not offend)	Use hand gestures that are specific to that culture (take caution to not offend)
It is ok to have a real hyped song to enter in on	Maybe skip the hype song. It is ok to ask the organizers of the event about their opinion.	Maybe skip the hype song. It is ok to ask the organizers of the event about their opinion.	Have a song based on the setting; it may be ok to incorporate music
Enter the stage pumped up and on fire. Be sure to focus on the content and not just on the hype.	The focus is more on the content vs the hype and cheer methods.	The focus is more on the content vs the hype and cheer methods.	Some hype is ok, and the focus is sometimes more on the content vs the hype and cheer methods.
High-five the audience	Greet the audience	Greet the audience	Varies depending on the event type
Run in	Walk in	Walk in	Varies depending on the event type
Scream your favorite word on your way onto the stage	Refrain depending on the event	Refrain depending on the event	Varies depending on the event type
Scream the name of the city you are in	Refrain depending on the event	Refrain depending on the event	Varies depending on the event type
Have a sincere look	Have a sincere look	Have a sincere look	Varies depending on the event type

POSITIVE

America	Europe	Asia	Africa
Walk tall, shoulders back	Walk tall, shoulders back	Walk tall, shoulders back	Varies depending on the event type
Have amazing energy	Have amazing energy	Have amazing energy	Varies depending on the event type
Wear bright clothing	Dress conservative	Dress conservative	Varies depending on the event type
Wear something crazy and exciting	Dress conservative	Dress conservative	Varies depending on the event type
Do a dance	Refrain depending on the event	Refrain depending on the event	Varies depending on the event type. Dance is welcomed in most African countries and event types.
Be happy and positive	Be happy and positive	Be happy and positive	Be happy and positive
Run a lap in the conference hall	Refrain depending on the event	Refrain depending on the event	Varies depending on the event type
Have your eyes wide open	Have your eyes wide open	Have your eyes wide open	Have your eyes wide open
Be yourself, be authentic	Be yourself, be authentic	Be yourself, be authentic	Be yourself, be authentic
Be careful with your choice of humor	Avoid humor if you are not a native, unless you are naturally funny	Avoid humor if you are not a native, unless you are naturally funny	Avoid humor if you are not a native, unless you are naturally funny
Do not talk about yourself when you first start speaking. No bragging, work comments about you into your talk versus a long list.	Do not talk about yourself when you first start speaking. No bragging, work comments about you into your talk versus a long list.	Do not talk about yourself when you first start speaking. No bragging, work comments about you into your talk versus a long list.	Do not talk about yourself when you first start speaking. No bragging, work comments about you into your talk versus a long list.

11 and 12

Pop and Pizzaz

It is time to show your true colors. Time to pop, time to shine, time to be yourself and show the world your unique flavor. Ice cream shops have multiple flavors. Most of them even have sprinkles, nuts, syrup, and all types of goodies for topping. Are you getting hungry yet? Let's shift from the example to its applicability to the book topic. Here is a question for you.

What is a characteristic that most every powerful speaker has? It is what I call pop. They have something that is the thing that makes them who they are AND makes them pop. Pop in this instance means stand out. Have you ever noticed that some people just have the IT FACTOR? The thing is though that everyone's IT FACTOR is different. Just like everyone's beauty is different. Some people see an ugly coat, and others think it is the best coat ever. Same with the pop idea. A loud and arm waving speaker could be the IT for some and be a turn off for others. Some have a soft voice, but their words are so impactful. They have the IT for some, and others might say, "I can barely hear them, this is boring." The thing with the IT is once you find what makes you pop, keep it and work it (Remembering to adapt it to the various cultures and countries you visit around the world as a global speaker.). Be you but with cultural sensitivities. I teach global thinking to students as part of my Echelon Leadership Academy. It is important for us as adults to all learn cultural sensitivities. One such case is when I went to Japan. As their special guest, it was their honor to have me eat first. Develop it and use it to the best of your abilities as often as possible. This is the thing that has made you stand out and you should be applauded for finding your IT. Monetize the heck out of your IT. Be crazy impactful with your IT. Thank your IT. I was communicating with someone today about their IT. Some people call it charisma. Other people call it personality. During public speaking and in life, there are some people that have the ability to draw you in no matter what it is that they're talking about.

This section has more to do with the overall package as opposed to just the person's speaking capability. The truth is some people were born with their personalities and ability to draw people in. For other people, it can be a learned skill but not always. How many people do you know that have spent hundreds or maybe even thousands of dollars in the hopes of mastering a certain skill? Some of them do succeed, yes. Oftentimes the instructor may actually be able to spot those who will succeed versus those who will have ongoing challenges.

Another viewpoint about pop and pizzazz is that everyone's style is not for everybody. This means everyone's speaking style or flavor is not for every listener. As a public speaker, it is up to you to decide whether you are speaking to appeal to the masses, or to a specific group of people. Just know that whoever you feel is the most powerful public speaker in the world, they are not everyone's cup of tea.

Let us take a moment before going to the next section to take a little quiz. Right down the name of the person that you feel is the most charismatic speaker. Now write down three reasons why you feel that way. Look at your list of three things and grade yourself based on where you are in your speaker's journey today. Keep this short list so you can come back to it later while reading this book. You can also go back to it and see what you wrote as you progress in your public speaking journey. That might be a month from now, three months from now, six months, or a year. It would be interesting to see what you put and how you progressed. Until then, keep popping.

13 and 14

Pupil and Pipes

A learner is a vessel of freedom.
A learner is a vessel of expansion.
A learner is a vessel of possibilities.
Are you a learner?
Are you able to use every experience as a learning opportunity?

My advice: Always be in learning mode. Always. Be the best student you know. Always. I am recommending this as a lifelong attitude. Be a sponge. Everywhere you go. Not just in a classroom setting. Every step you take and every breath you breathe is an opportunity to be in learning mode. Be a student and build your mindset, skill, and wisdom.

Some may have been in a car accident or may have had a stroke or other medical condition. In these cases, public speaking would mean speaking in general. Learning to speak again could be something that takes time. In this section, I am going to address speaking from a re-learning perspective. Some may need speech therapy due to some of the things I mentioned earlier. If this is the case, here is a list to address some of the speaking lessons that can be gleaned from this book.

Use this book to find the value-added elements that are right for you or your patient if you are a medical professional.

Outline the value-added sections in an order that makes sense based on the type of speech training or re-learning that is needed.

Start slow, not putting too much pressure through the vocal cords. This can cause further vocal cord dysfunction, paralysis, and damage.

If a person is re-learning to speak in general, start with small one- or two-syllable words that do not cause too much pressure.

In these cases, coughing can also cause pain or sore throat episodes.

Keep the throat moist and avoid irritation.

Do like the greats. Powerful public speakers do what they need to do to protect their pipes (e.g., your vocal cords). Some use honey to coat their throat. Others use room temperature water, warm water, cough drops, lemon water, steam, and more.

Our pipes can make us a living.

Our pipes are the main instrument of our profession.

Our pipes need to be nurtured and maintained.

Our pipes can fatigue, so use them with purpose.

15

Performance

It is time for lights, camera, and action.

This is true every day. After all, life is one big stage, do you agree or disagree?

Let's face it. Some are on stage just to perform. Some are there to have impact. Some want to be noticed. For those who are into public speaking for the right reasons, there is still an element of performing.

In every performance, there are numerous dynamics. These are the things that make the performance worth watching. It has highs and lows of lighting, voice intonations, wardrobe changes, musical numbers, maybe even some smoke coming from the right or left wing, the lines spoken by the performers pull at the heart strings of the audience, connecting on multiple levels emotionally and intellectually, and, last but not least, let us not forget the dancers. Everything is precisely planned and executed to give the audience the experience of a lifetime, one that they will discuss for years to come.

This is the case if the performance was dynamic enough to draw that kind of feeling and connection. So, it is for our speaking engagements. The truth is that you may not have music, dancers, and lighting changes in your talks, but you can paint a picture so vivid with your words that those listening in feel like they are in a full motion picture as you take them from scene to scene with your words, diction, use of the full stage or speaking area, complete with hand gestures, soft and loud volume and more. Let us not leave all of the fun for the theatrical performers. Let's use their cues and incorporate some of their engaging secrets in our public speaking and see how they just might turn you into a world-class speaker yet.

So, here is a summary of some of the visualizations from above. Think about how you can use some of these in your next talk, either physically or by painting mental pictures.

Consider your:

- Use of the stage or speaking area
- Lighting
- Volume and pitch
- Props and wardrobe
- Emotional connection
- Heartstring connection

I have heard many public speakers mention that they are not there to entertain. The truth is, whilst most speeches will be entertaining, all speeches must be engaging and empowering. There has to be an element of performing, just from the perspective of keeping the attention of the audience. This does not mean that you need to go way far out away from your authentic character. Anything you do, after all, must be where you can do it and feel good about your actions. Feeling like you were a complete phony is no way to live.

Percent

The average person laughs about seventeen times a day with the range going from 0 to 80 (per swnsdigital.com).

One out of ten people are likely to fulfill their self-imposed new year's resolutions, according to another study.

Numbers.

They help us understand the underlying thoughts, opinions, and moods of people all over the world.

Using stats…

Everyone that knows me knows that I love data. I love statistics. I'm a geek about understanding the thought process and philosophy behind whatever topic I'm speaking about. It is also my opinion that everyone would be wise to want to do the same. Research is key. Understanding how many people have been uplifted and encouraged related to a certain topic is just as important as those who have experienced difficulty. For instance, one statistic that I give is about the percentage of people with anxiety and depression disorders. This is very key because many people have never even felt that they could fulfill their dreams in life because they let life weigh them down before they even get to the good part. This is also related to mindset. Anything that deals with the human thought process's underlying condition and what helps people experience freedom or not is essential to me.

For this section, I recommend that you at least have two or three sets of data to share during your talk, depending on the length of the address.

If it is short, meaning around five to ten minutes, you may want to keep your statistical references to one. Find one thing that you wish the hearers to wrap their minds around. Sometimes people use this as an opener, meaning, this is the first thing that they say. Sometimes people don't even give their name; they go right on stage and say, "did you know"... then they go into a short story about it. Then they say their name and give more information about what they're going to talk about. This is an attention grabber because now the audience hopefully is intrigued. Hopefully, I say, because sometimes people have not read their audience or did not understand who they were speaking to make the statistic relevant. Having relevant data based on your audience is also imperative.

Another thing related to statistics and data is that you could take something that seems like it does not connect and find a relation. I love doing this as part of live training with speakers and potential speakers. For instance, there could be a paperclip on the table. I have everyone look at the paperclip. Then I'll give them a particular topic. The participants are then given the challenge to relate that paperclip to that topic. Why don't you try it out? Let's say the matter is humanity. So, I ask you, how can you do a five-minute talk relating that paperclip to humankind. I would love to hear what you have to say on that. Feel free to send your paperclip and humanity write-up to me via my website **https://krystyllerichardson.com**

For the last comment in this section, I would like to use the word imperative again. It is essential and imperative to give credit to the organization or person whose data you are citing. If you use a statistic and go over specific percentages and details related to a study, do not say it so that it makes it seem like it's your research. I love data so much that I have started a data collection and resource organization to help speakers gather and have more information about their unique topic. There will be more information on the website www.statscollective.com. Remember at the beginning of this section, I said that I love data. Oh,

I indeed do. Many of the speakers around the world who do very well help draw their audience and are viewed as the authority in that area, the expert. Data helps to lay the foundation for that. Don't be afraid to do the research and use data often to get your point across. Another caution is don't go down the rabbit hole and gather too much data. Then you're spouting off percentages about this and about that and confusing your audience. They don't want to necessarily feel like they're in a college or university lecture. But they do want to know that they are not alone based on a particular thought or feeling. Going over percentages sometimes helps people feel like they are part of a larger group. Meaning, oh, there are other people out there that have experienced the same thing that I have.

I look forward to hearing your stories. Also include in it one statistic and how it relates to the paper clip and humanity. Before you forget a few things, you may have thought of already on this, I will include a notes page right here in case you have a great idea for this.

REFLECTIONS
Humanity notes

_____
_____
_____
_____
_____
_____
_____
_____
_____
_____
_____
_____
_____
_____
_____
_____
_____
_____
_____
_____

You can grab the full and complete workbook to accompany this book by visiting **https://krystyllerichardson.com/51Psworkbook**

NOTES and MAKE UP YOUR OWN MIND

ACTION PLAN

Issue: _____
_____
_____
_____

Why should I work on this? _____
_____
_____
_____

What is my desired outcome? _____
_____
_____
_____

Steps to work on this – list top 3 to 5 steps: _____
_____
_____
_____
_____
_____
_____

This must be done by (timeframe/date): _____

_____

_____

If this does not happen, what is the negative effect: _____

_____

_____

_____

_____

I proclaim that I will: _____

_____

_____

_____

_____

_____

_____

_____

_____

_____

> "Data gives your speech power. Use that power wisely. Not too much, not too little."
>
> **Krystylle Richardson**

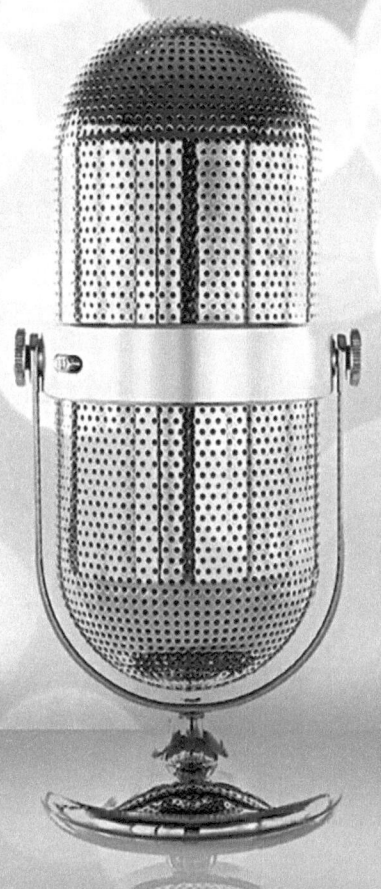

"Public speaking is an art. Utilize your tapestry well, incorporating both grace and innovation."

Krystylle Richardson

Pose

Left, right, stop and turn.
Hand up, hand out, arms crossed and stop.

Models do this every day. As a speaker, do you know the context of pose?

This is such a beautiful word and has such an excellent context. Pose. Why do I feel that it has a beautiful context? I'm glad you asked. I teach dance, and part of what we do is making sure that we have various moments in which our stance is memorable. So, we're making pictures with our bodies at various points in time, not just doing movements. Some of them are forward-facing, some to the side, some to the back. The point is to do something that has remarkable speeds fast and slow. Also, do things where your body is up or down. This means that you have variety. Sometimes the body is in a diagonal of some sort. With some of the movements being fast or slow, you can draw attention to a specific action by slowing down or even stopping before you go to the next beat. The same thing is true when you pose during public speaking. Let's dig into this further.

During public speaking, you want to give your audience variety. You don't want to just stand in one spot with your body position or one spot with your voice. So, pose, in my opinion, has to do with both. What are some positions that you can do to get the attention of your audience? For this one, I'm going to go into a little bit more detail related to some of your main body parts as well as your voice.

Head and shoulders

If we look at the word pose related to your head and shoulders, there's one very clear thing. Most of the people's attention when you're speaking in public is directed towards your head, correct? The answer is yes. Also, your shoulders play a big part in that as well. So, if your head is leaning from side to side or bouncing up and down, or your head is up too high, that can throw off your speaking event. People will not be focused on the content of what you're saying but rather on your head's awkward and distracting position—the same thing for your shoulders. If your shoulders are hunched up, then that can be distracting. What you can do with your head and shoulders has to do with what you're speaking about. If you're talking about going from the beginning or end of something, or a starting line and a finishing line, you can move your head to the right and to the left to simulate the position of start to finish from left to right. This helps to give a visual for the audience—the same thing for using your shoulders. You can pose so one second, two, three, four seconds with your shoulders up to draw attention to the shoulder shrug as part of what it is that you're speaking about. Sometimes, a shoulder shrug is used to say, "I don't know." Using your body during your speaking brings life to your speech. You don't want to overdo it, but it helps bring flavor and style to what you're saying.

Can you think of any ways to use your head and shoulders that would be good based on the topic you want to speak about? Feel free to write down some of your creative ideas below.

_____

_____

_____

_____

POSE

You can grab the full and complete workbook to accompany this book by visiting
https://krystyllerichardson.com/51Psworkbook

Get creative

Back

Having a straight back, meaning you're standing up straight, is another portion of the very important pose. Walking around hunched over can again be distracting. If it's being done to draw attention to what you're speaking about, as mentioned before, that's a different story. During public speaking, it is important to have a straight back, in my opinion, because it helps you look more confident and more like an authoritative figure. After all, part of what you're trying to do when you speak most times is to help people understand that you're an expert or an authority or have knowledge and wisdom related to whatever the topic is. If you have poor posture, then that can spoil your whole speech.

Can you think of any ways to use your back that would be good based on the topic you want to speak about? Feel free to write down some of your creative ideas below.

_____
_____
_____
_____
_____
_____
_____
_____
_____
_____

Arms and hands

I love this part of the book and the explanation that goes forth, especially in this section related to the pose. Your arms and hands are another part of your body that we can use based on the word pose. Making a muscle to show that you're strong or that the person should be strong is a good use of your arms. Shaking your arms to express shaking something off is also a good way to use your arms to get the point across. Moving your hand or your fingers around in a circle to show that something is going on and on and on is another option. Counting out '1, 2, 3' with your fingers is another good use of your hands. This helps give the audience a visual of which point or fact that you are on. Meaning, what concept are you going over: the first one, the second one, the third one, and so on. Leaving your hand in the air with your arm going back and forth can show that you're speaking about getting someone's attention. You can also put your hand up to show that you want someone to stop something. You can clap your hands; you can bang one hand in the palm of the other hand. You can rub your hands together as the emotion of being devious is a part of your speech. The options here are endless on ways to use your hands and your arms.

Can you think of any ways to use your hands and arms that would be good based on the topic you want to speak about? Feel free to write down some of your creative ideas below.

_____

_____

_____

_____

_____

Legs and feet

Now it's time to get moving. Use those legs and use those feet to move in ways that make sense during your speaking. This does not mean to pace back and forth. This is one of the common mistakes that public speakers make where they think that that brings flavor to their talk when it just makes people feel like they're watching a tennis match. Your movement should be intentional.

When I'm on stage, where am I speaking from? Meaning, is the podium in the middle of the stage on the side, or is there no podium? Do I have on a lapel mic or a handheld mic? Microphones will be covered in a different section. This comment was only stated as a correlation.

Are there some dance moves you can incorporate into your speech? What about moving amongst the audience?

Can you think of any ways to use your legs and feet that would be good based on the topic you want to speak about? Feel free to write down some of your creative ideas below.

_____
_____
_____
_____
_____
_____
_____
_____
_____

"Your poses add spice and flavor to your public speaking. So, strike a pose and mean it. Use that power wisely. Draw your audience in with your unique movement and flare."

Krystylle Richardson

NOTES and MAKE UP YOUR OWN MIND

ACTION PLAN

Issue: _____
_____
_____
_____

Why should I work on this? _____
_____
_____
_____

What is my desired outcome? _____
_____
_____
_____

Steps to work on this – list top 3 to 5 steps: _____
_____
_____
_____
_____
_____

This must be done by (timeframe/date): _____

_____

_____

If this does not happen, what is the negative effect: _____

_____

_____

_____

_____

I proclaim that I will: _____

_____

_____

_____

_____

_____

_____

_____

_____

_____

_____

Introducing ...

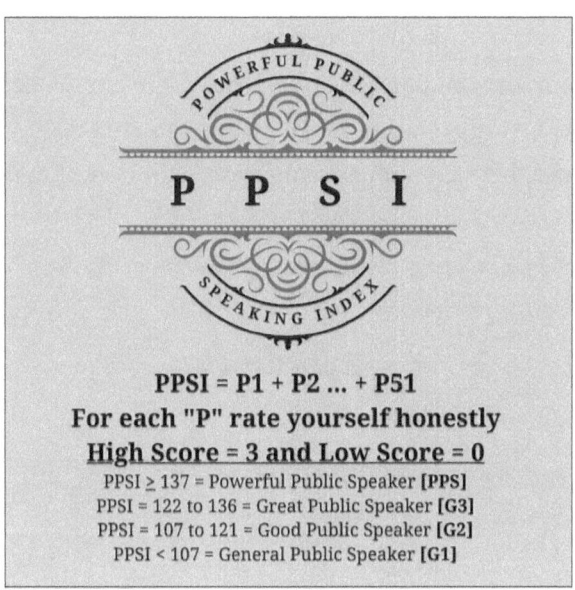

The Powerful Public Speaking Index ™

How to know if you are a powerful public speaker.

There are many opinions floating around the atmosphere regarding the answer to this question.

For instance, here are some opinions on public speaking:

Wherever I go meeting the public... spreading a message of human values, spreading a message of harmony, is the most important thing.

Dalai Lama

The critic has to educate the public; the artist has to educate the critic.

Oscar Wilde

The flowery style is not unsuitable to public speeches or addresses, which amount only to compliment. The lighter beauties are in their place when there is nothing more solid to say; but the flowery style ought to be banished from a pleading, a sermon, or a didactic work.

Voltaire

The time comes upon every public man when it is best for him to keep his lips closed.

Abraham Lincoln

Based on this, I have also taken the liberty to throw my hat in the ring so to speak and give my take on it. A powerful public speaker is one who has impact, period. It has nothing to do with being well known, a person of monetary wealth, a person of high regard amongst people, a person of tall stature or eloquence of speech. It has to do with impact. It has nothing to do with how many people were present during the speaking event. Whether there were 2 or 2,000 or 20,000, it does not matter. Whether the person got a standing ovation or silence during and after the speaking event does not matter. Impact is what matters. For me, knowing that I had a positive effect on at least one person's life is a big factor. I do strive to affect as many as I can so that they can in turn go on to affect many people, spreading positivity and impact further than I could ever do alone. Achieving what I call connectivity impact is what is important to me. That being said, I have devised a way to measure how powerful a speaker is. I do this based on the use of a trademarked index that I developed after hearing thousands of speeches from people of numerous countries, ages, ethnicities, social standing and more. I study people, and always have.

This index is called the **PPSI ™**, or **Powerful Public Speaking Index**™.

Although there really is no way to know what one person truly feels is powerful versus another, I do sincerely feel that this PPSI rating gives a good indication that a person is well on their way to becoming a powerful public speaker. The way to use it is to understand the foundational premise of honesty.

In order for any rating system to give you the biggest reward or view of a situation, there must be a good solid and honest view of the subject matter. In this case, if you are rating yourself, it could be more difficult.

Some of us have an inflated view of ourselves. Others of us are always hard on ourselves. Obviously, this means that others are in the middle somewhere. Let's have fun though and learn this index and use it on ourselves AND to evaluate a few of the great speakers that are in your circle.

Do they utilize any or all of the 51 Powerful Ps? If they utilize others that are not noted in this book, I would love to hear about them.

Contact me at krystyllerichardson.com and share.

We will likely have continued editions of this book and we could update our listings accordingly if your new Ps will be value added to our readers.

Now let's jump into the PPSI, shall we?

Here is the general overview of the index and how the scoring works.

Decide to utilize the checklist of the 51 Powerful Ps. Use the rating system of 3 being the highest score and 0 being the lowest. Do not allow your mind to get overwhelmed by there being 51 areas to evaluate. Focus on the end goal, being a better public speaker.

Next, read the section of this book that pertains to the Powerful P to be rated, then assign a score in the checklist. Copy this scoring page and use it as often as needed. Pick a few of the Powerful Ps to score yourself on and also record the date. Study more on the Powerful P's. Practice some of them by yourself and with family and friends. Maybe even practice some of them during a podcast or small speaking event. Write your score and as stated remember to record the date. Do this every month or after every practice. Is your score getting better each time? If yes great. Do not be too hard on yourself but do be honest with yourself. Self-honesty during this evaluation is a must. I would love to hear about your progress. Feel free to send an update or two to the contact section of krystyllerichardson.com. The goal is to know where you are starting from, then determine what is needed to increase your knowledge and skill to get to the next level. Coaches help with this. Practice is your biggest weapon and tool. Nothing can propel you further than DOING. The key is doing what you need to do, with a plan and a clear understanding of the desired end result. It is very important to know where you are, what you need to do, and where you want to go. Understanding how to outline an improvement plan using these three concepts will allow you to grow leaps and bounds. Using a system to learn and assess progress wins over scattered, haphazard approaches every time.

Now that we have learned a bit about the PPSI ™, let us go back and use it to evaluate Power Positions 1, 2, and 3. For Power Position 4, 5, and 6 the scoring block will be right after the chapters.

> You can grab the full and complete workbook to accompany this book by visiting
> https://krystyllerichardson.com/51Psworkbook

How To Know If You Are A Powerful Public Speaker.

Powerful Practice Groupings

Stop where you are in this book. Time to practice.
Pick 3 of the Powerful Public Speaking Ps
Write what it is about these 3 that you want to perfect
Practice 7 times over a set period of time
Each time, take notes and adjust as needed
Determine your score or have others determine a score
Are you getting better each time?

Powerful Public Speaking P Date: Practice # :	Score (1-10)
1.	
2.	
3.	

Powerful Practice Groupings

Stop where you are in this book. Time to practice.
Pick 3 of the Powerful Public Speaking Ps
Write what it is about these 3 that you want to perfect
Practice 7 times over a set period of time
Each time, take notes and adjust as needed
Determine your score or have others determine a score
Are you getting better each time?

	Powerful Public Speaking P Date: Practice # :	Score (1-10)
1.		
2.		
3.		

Powerful Practice Groupings

Stop where you are in this book. Time to practice.
Pick 3 of the Powerful Public Speaking Ps
Write what it is about these 3 that you want to perfect
Practice 7 times over a set period of time
Each time, take notes and adjust as needed
Determine your score or have others determine a score
Are you getting better each time?

	Powerful Public Speaking P Date: Practice # :	Score (1-10)
1.		
2.		
3.		

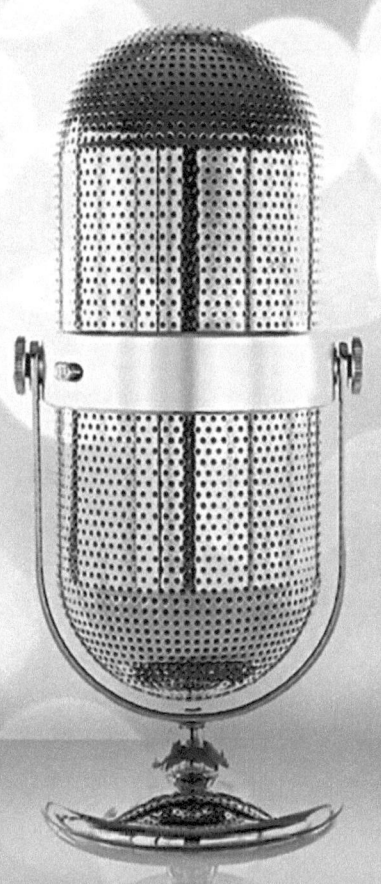

"The beauty of a prelude is that it sets up the palate of the mind's eye to anxiously await the main course. The prelude is the foreplay to the yum."

Krystylle Richardson

Power

Let's get excited together.
    Let's celebrate you.
Let's celebrate your power.
Yes you.
You are a powerful being.
You have the power to move minds.
You have the power to move attitudes.
You have the power to move nations.
You have the power to build companies.
You have the power to create laughter.
You have the power to invoke anger.
You have the power to bring people to tears.
And yet, so many do not understand that they have power at all.
That ends today.
So, just as in the section related to push, which is to power up and stay high, I want to talk about the word power by itself. During your talk, you must come with power. That does not mean that you need to yell and scream your words at the audience. That is one misconception that people have about the word power. It can be a person with the sincerest voice that does not have much volume to it that is the most powerful speaker you may have ever heard. Why is that? It's because of their content. They had content that came with impact. They had content that came with conviction. They had content that came with you

listening to it and knowing right away that you need to make a change in your life. So, I ask you, do you understand the word power? Have you spoken with power in your voice? Do you use volume to show power, or do you use impact to show power? I love this word. That may be evident because this book's name is the 51 Powerful Ps of Public Speaking. I have interviewed and been in the presence of hundreds of powerful public speakers. Some of them just so happen to be millionaires and billionaires. Some of them are pastors. Some of them are housewives. It does not matter the status of the person. What matters is impact. As you may tell by now, I equate the word impact with power. I do not equate the word power with volume.

Think of a power lifter. Some of them do a grunt, or they do something to release from their voice as they're lifting something heavy. Others may keep it in, and you may see their neck get bigger, their jaws get bigger, and their face gets red. You may even see their hands shake, or their knees shake. There's a lot of power that's going on to lift those weights. So, whether they're a screamer or whether they keep it internal, you can still see and feel the power. So, I do not want you to equate power to one type or one way to look at this word.

Let's look at another sport, golf. You can walk up to the ball on the tee and have in the back of your mind that you're going to kill that ball with your club. You line up the club with the ball, and your backswing takes place. You then use all of your might to swing that club to hit the ball, thinking that all of that power will make it go far. That is not always the case. Some of the people who have the best golf shots use the power of their minds. They use all of the training that they were given, all of their practice, to do all of the movements in a way that brings power by using their whole body as a well-oiled machine. That golfer sometimes hits the ball, and their swing does not indicate that that ball will go far at all. But it does. Why is that?

Because they use their mind. They use their practice. They use everything that they were trained to use. So based on that example, I want to ask you a question. What training have you done for public speaking? What practice have you done? All of that leads to power. When you've practiced, and when you've been coached, and when you know what you need to say and how you need to say it, all of those can help you have a powerful talk. You can be using your mind to survey the audience and figure out ways to bring more power instead of using your mind to remember the words you're going to say. The words will just flow if you put the proper preparation in place. I love this quote and feel that it fits here:

> ***You learn to speak by speaking, to study by studying, to run by running, to work by working; in just the same way, you learn to love by loving.***
>
> *Anatole France*

So, let's practice all of the 51 Ps of powerful public speaking; let's continue to read about some of the examples of powerful speakers and come up with the game plan on how we want to be viewed when we speak. It is time for you to speak with power. Are you ready?

Point

Count them.
 Empower your audience with them.
Don't shy away from them.
Be bold in your selection of them.
All famous stories have them. All audiences remember the talks that have clear ones.
What was the point of making the Mona Lisa?
What was the point and back story of why a mother decides to have a child?
One of the things that are always very fun when someone is speaking is trying to pick out their key points. Sometimes people say '1, 2, 3' and sometimes they don't. Even though I said that that's sometimes fun, it can be, or the alternative is that it makes you lose your audience. Before we go on in the section discussing points, keep in mind that less is better. If you have one main idea for people to focus on, then great.

If that one idea has one to three points to consider, then also great. The more points you chose to state, the less they may remember. With that said, let's get into how to use this section based on the style and purpose of your talk. You should never have your audience keeping track of seven steps for this or five keys of that; it should be very clear to your audience. Using the word point, don't keep them waiting and guessing with a lot of flowery stories. Get to the point. Also, state which point you're on. If you sometimes have problems remembering what point you're on, have a cheat sheet. Something to help take off that you're done with one, done with point two, and so on. Sometimes students get very frustrated when they are really into what you're saying, but you said you were on points 1, 2, 3 and to point 4, and then you say on to point 7. That leaves your student or audience saying, what the heck just happened? Did I just fall asleep and miss points 4, 5, and 6? Do I raise my hand and ask the question or let it go?

Don't keep your audience guessing. Don't confuse your audience by skipping points and not remembering your points. Stay on point. It is also good sometimes to give them a bonus point or fact. An example is, if you say you're giving seven points, you might want to say, and here's another one that is helpful that I'll give you as a bonus or for free. Then, go on to say your next point. People love bonuses and thinking that they're getting extra. So, give your audience a gift and always think about doing some kind of bonus.

Another way to handle this is in relation to the amount of time you're using doing your talk. If there's no one that's going to be after you or if you were the only speaker, you and the audience know what will happen next. If you're talking and supposed to be over at 4:00 p.m., as an example, you can ask them if anyone is interested in spending thirty more minutes digging deeper into the topic. I've seen this done during a number of talks. If the audience is engaged, they will gladly stay to pick up a few more nuggets, a few more points. As the speaker, you should be able to gauge this. Make sure that you keep a pulse on your interest. One way to do this is to ask a few people during break time or during your session. Doing it this way helps you to be able to ask the question about them wanting more points and having a positive outcome.

- Step 1: Pick 5 people to hear you do a 2-minute talk.
- Step 2: Ask them to take notes.
- Step 3: Do the talk.
- Step 4: Ask for written feedback — short — in general regarding what your main points were.
- Step 5: Thank them.
- Step 6: Review the input, did they write down the points that you were trying the make?
- Step 7: Make corrections in your talk as needed.
- Step 8: Perfect your craft as the world's next most powerful public speaker.

You can grab the full and complete workbook to accompany this book by visiting
https://krystyllerichardson.com/51Psworkbook

"If you are lost in your talk and don't even get the point, how can your audience? Clear points need to transform your audience. Transformation can lead to impact in the lives of those who understood your points, and cash in your pocket if you are aspiring to be a paid speaker."

Krystylle Richardson

20

Promise

How important is a promise? A father and son are on a park bench. The son asks to play catch when they get home. The father agrees. Once they are home the father gets a phone call and then gets busy with other things. The son watches the father for the rest of the evening to see if it is time to go out to play catch. The father goes and goes the rest of the evening after the phone call and does not remember until it is now 10p.m. The father is now embarrassed and is also tired. With the remembrance of the sons face in his head from the park bench, he gets convicted. The son is now sleep. The father still goes to the son's room, sees that he is sleep, and stands watching him dream. The father decides to go ahead and wake him up. When the son opens his eyes, the father has the baseball gloves in his hands and had written a note that said, "sorry son." The next note he showed him said "are you ready for a nighttime catch session?" The son rubs his eyes, smiles and gets out of bed, to go out in the dark night sky and play catch with his dad. The boy was smiling the whole time, and so was the dad. The promise had been fulfilled. Although late, it was still fulfilled.

Sometimes what we promise goes as planned and other times it may take a turn; the important thing is to keep that promise. Now let's relate this to our public speaking powers.

Promise keepers are respected in the long run. Whoever has the mic has the power. That is something that is said from time to time during public speaking. Whoever has the mic also is the person who can make promises to the audience. Here is where this section becomes more important. If you say something in life and when you're on the mic, it is important that you keep whatever promises have been made. Suppose you tell your audience that you're going to give them access to a chapter of your book, you need to make sure that you do it. If you guarantee your audience that they will get a specific result based on implementing five steps that you have, for instance, then it should be that that is true as well. The point of this section is to make sure that you keep your promises. Sometimes, we're so quick to get caught up in the moment that we say things that are true, partially true, funny, but not necessarily true, and the list could go on and on. The other part is that sometimes we get carried away with offering things that we don't have.

Based on some of the comments that I've stated above, hopefully, you get the picture. This has been something that I've seen in conferences before, and afterward, it is not a pretty picture. This could show up on a speaker evaluation or event evaluation. If those are not offered as something that the conference wants you to do, it might show up in comments on Facebook or other social media outlets. You have now developed a reputation for being a speaker who makes promises that are empty. If something happens in your life as a life event that has caused a delay in whatever it is that you have promised, that is a different story. For instance, I contracted the COVID-19 virus months ago, which put me behind on many things that I was doing. It has been very difficult to get everything caught up, and sometimes I feel more and more behind each day. One thing is true though, I'm glad that I'm still alive and glad that I feel better. I still have my good days and bad days, but I try to be open about that. Some people like to keep things private. It kind of depends on the situation. In this case, I'm very open with the people I'm working with that I'm still trying to dig myself out. I do a lot of apologizing for things that are late or very extremely behind and hope that they hear and feel the sincerity in my voice. This is a bit different than promising things from the stage. Still, I think it should be clear by now what the point is. If you cannot deliver it, don't promise it from the stage.

21

Paid

Do you like music? I do. Out of all of the songs out there, we are going to look at a particular type of song. There are lots of songs in the world about money. There are songs about getting paid. Let's have a look into the public speaking world in relation to getting paid.

If you've been looking around in the public speaking space, you know by now that there are various types of speakers. This book would not be complete if I didn't just take a moment to go over several of them. We don't need to spend a lot of time on it, but we do need to cover it to ensure you have the basics of the various types. They have many names, and I will use some familiar descriptions as well; it's something that may be a bit more colorful.

Here is my list of the various types of public speakers. Any one of these categories could be a paid or nonpaid talk. Part of the key is knowing your worth. This is all based on your audience and understanding their needs, and how you connect. This section, however, is to talk about the types of speakers. But all of these types of speakers have gotten speaking engagements. Will you be one of them?

Let's go to the list.

The following is not a comprehensive list but one that I wanted to highlight today. We will pick several of them to dig a little deeper into the particulars of that type of speaker:

- Transformational
- Motivational

- Inspirational
- Informational
- Soapbox
- Monologue
- Purpose-driven
- Interactive
- Speak to enroll
- Storyteller
- Activist
- Testimonial Speaker
- Panelist Speaker
- Guest Speaker
- Keynote Speaker

Some people speak to be seen. Some speak to be heard. Some speak to be felt. Others speak to be believed. Some speak for impact.

My question to you is what do you want people to say after they hear you speak?

- He was an amazing speaker.
- He had so much power.
- Her talk changed my life.
- I'm not sure I remember anything that she said.
- Were you bored with his talk? I was too, let's go shopping.
- That was a waste of brain cells.
- I cannot believe I agreed to sit through that for an hour.
- I'm so glad I took notes. I'm going to review them over and over again.
- This talk came at just the right time in my life.
- I was not expecting that he was phenomenal.
- I wonder how much they paid that speaker to speak? I would pay myself. This talk was such a game-changer for me.

- I wonder how much they paid that speaker to speak? They should be paying me to listen.

This list could go on and on, but I think you get the point. People are going to have some type of reaction after your talk. Sometimes this reaction comes even after the first ten seconds of you speaking.

Keep in mind that it is an honor for people to listen to you. They could be doing lots of other things with their time and their money. So let us all make sure that we're doing the best that we can to understand our audience and match our message up so that we have amazing life-changing type comments and not the kind that mentioned a ridiculous use of time.

- Step 1: Pick 5 of your favorite speakers.
- Step 2: Define which type of speaker they are.
- Step 3: Pick a short speech or talk from them.
- Step 4: Evaluate that speech based on a few of the Ps in this book.
- Step 5: Determine what they might be able to improve.
- Step 6: Learn from their high and low scores.
- Step 7: Perfect your craft as the world's next most powerful public speaker.

You can grab the full and complete workbook to accompany this book by visiting
https://krystllerichardson.com/51Psworkbook

22

Price

A bottle of water in one scenario can cost ten "huntrees" (this is our fictious currency division). In another case that same bottle of water could cost thirty huntrees. In a big sports event, that same bottle of water could have the price of it raised to fifty huntrees. That same bottle could be only five huntrees in a rural area where there is less demand for it. The point is, it is the same bottle, it is just in different settings. This is the same regarding you and public speaking pricing.

What price did you pay to be where you are today? As you go further into the Prelude Power Position, start thinking about price. Start thinking about the price of your offer if you are a conference speaker.

In the previous section, you read about PAID and the types of paid speakers. Now let's start thinking about your price if you are sending in a quote for a speaking spot where you get paid upfront. Start thinking about how to baseline your pricing. Some have said they think about what the price should be and double it. Some think about the audience and discount it.

This is an area where you truly have to do what you feel is best and learn from every lesson that comes from it. No one has walked in your shoes. No one knows your motives. People do however know if you are underpricing yourself.

You may want to agree to a percentage of the ticket sales if the organization you are speaking for is selling tickets and does not have much money, giving them a minimum amount to cover, such as your expenses.

People will have opinions, and since this is my book, here is my expert advice:

Food on the table is better than no food. If you need to offer a slightly lower price to get food, do it. This means, if you want to offer them your speaking services for a lower price you can do so; however, do not state it as a discount. State it as a 'limited time offer' or price for women entrepreneurs or give some reason. After you get on your feet, raise your prices. You owe it to yourself and those counting on you. Another way to do the pricing is to ask them if they have a budget for their event, and what did they budget for a speaker. You can then write the full amount on the invoice, cross it out and put their budget amount if you so choose. Another option is to research the organization. Who have they had as speakers before? Review the websites of the previous speakers and see if they have a fee listed. If they do and it is higher than yours and you have comparable experience, raise your price. I had a school tell me that WHEN they invite me back the next year to double my price. I did. They paid. All went well.

Never forget your worth. It is ok to take steps to get there, but always have your worth in mind, backed by what you know you can deliver. Write your keynote price on your vision board and work towards that under a specific timeframe. Once you are there, compare the dates, did you get there early, or did it take a few more years? Once there, feel free to stay at the amount for a while, and then raise it if you are so inclined. This is not just to make more money, but you could also let the program coordinators know what you do from a philanthropy perspective, and that donations will be made to charities based on their generosity. You decide your angle. Just remember to not do it for greed but have a purpose for the raised price. A lot went into you getting to where you are today as a speaker. It is ok to be paid for it. It is also ok to do some speaking engagements out of the kindness of your heart, you decide. Power comes in authenticity, and not in chasing the dollar.

23

Partner

The saying that we are better together holds true in most cases.

This is also true for public speaking.

The prelude is such an important position in this book. It is where all of the magic happens to put you well on your way to being more powerful. Partnering is one way to support those goals. Some people may get to this section and ask what does partnering have to do with public speaking? My answer is a lot. There are various levels of partnering that I want to touch on. The first one has to do with your practice. Partnering up with someone else who is also on your same journey is always good. Having an accountability partner gives you the support that you need to get better. This isn't the same as a coach or a mentor. It is strictly a person who can help you based on listening to you practice a speech, for instance. If it is someone who is in your industry, then that's where partnering helps because they may be willing to give you some suggestions on some words that could be changed. If you both have this book, for instance, you could use it to evaluate what things they need to work on based on hints from the book. You could also use the flash cards.

Another form of partnering might have to do with conferences. If you're going to be speaking at a conference and you know one or two or five or six others that are going to be speaking there as well, then you have a ready-made support team. Navigating all of the ins and outs and technical issues for virtual conferences can sometimes be overwhelming. Just know that you don't have to go it alone. Reach out and ask people for support. Maybe even make a message group on text or Facebook or Instagram, or wherever you would like. This way, all of you can learn the ins and outs together and save one another some heartaches related to the speaking engagement.

Of course, it's not where you want to go through your full talk with someone else, hearing all your main points before you get on stage. Some people are okay with that; it just depends on your preference. This also helps if you want to get additional pictures and videos of you speaking. Those people can be positioned in various places around the auditorium or conference room.

Now you have your camera crew to get some really good media assets for you to use later. It doesn't even matter if the pictures, audio, or video are good quality. You would hope that they would be, but even if they aren't, there are all kinds of filters and editing options available to you to bring out what you need in order to use them as media assets.

You also have people then that will clap for you or raise their hand if you're asking questions. This shows support for you, and other people might clap just because of the other person. One of the points that I am writing about here is that relationships matter. I've said in this book already that you don't need to go it alone. This could be another Powerful P, actually. Plants. Think about it and you decide.

Powerful public speakers have power because they motivate people. So, in this case, use the power of partnering and make your next speaking engagement the best one ever. Built-in support is sometimes the best support.

24

Polite

He was so nice, the woman mentioned after hearing a man talking about his mother on the train. He exhibited care and compassion when he spoke about the story of his mother and her trip to pick out roses for her rose garden. It was a delight to listen in on the story as we all were riding the train to go to our respective places that morning. Let us know relate this to public speaking.

Why are manners important when you speak? I am quite sure that all of us have heard speakers who are not so polite, ones who thrive on being brash, rude, and controversial. Sometimes these speakers are up in the faces of their audience, giving them either solicited or unsolicited advice or wisdom.

Be that as it may, even in those cases I would say that there is still a sense of politeness going on. This word can go from "Yes ma'am," "No ma'am" to "Yes sir," "Please," and "Thank you," to other forms. Sometimes in the brash cases, a person may seem rude, but in reality, they are polite in the ways that matter. Just like all parts of this book, it is up to you if you will apply these tools or not.

Here is a list of the ways that I feel that being polite can help you as a public speaker:

Polite to those who helped with the stage set up for your talk.

Polite to the program managers and MC personnel who keep things moving.

Polite to the person who will introduce you.

Polite to the other speakers that are a part of that particular platform or business location.

Polite to all that are on the audio and visual production team helping with the mics, lighting, etc.

Polite to the audience based on your style of speaking.

Polite to the stage crew.

All of these are also known as gratitude, and when you are a grateful speaker, the host is grateful to you and more willing to book you again or refer you. That doesn't mean you can get away with delivering a bad speech and wrap it up in gratitude, nor does it suggest offering politeness and gratitude, but as the saying goes, "Manners maketh man," including woman.

Plagiarism

A teacher at a university was explaining three ways that the students could go about developing a story line for an upcoming competition. He had the students raise their hands and gave three of them different cards to teach his point on how to develop this particular part of the story. The cards said:

- I wrote that. I spoke about it.
- I referenced that in my talk.
- I took that. I spoke about it and did not give credit to the writer.

He then went on to work with the three students to show how this could be verbalized in their talks and how this could demonstrate his point on this key word that we will explore in this section of this book, plagiarism.

You may be asking why is this word in this book? After all, plagiarism is bad right? The short answer is yes. The longer answer is, not in the manner that I am about to explain.

Admiring those who have inspired you to become a powerful person of impact is awesome. So how do you do that?

There is no need to keep you in suspense as to how this can be ok. So here it is. Playful plagiarism is what I am calling my point in this section of the book. Here is an example. If you really like a phrase or a concept that a person has said in the past and want to playfully use it as your own (only for a moment), in my opinion, that is okay. There may likely be member of your audience that actually knows the quote and will know that it is not yours. The playful way might be to say that "A great leader once said 'xyz' and that great leader was me." Then after a few moments say, "Just kidding, that is a tremendously helpful and impactful quote by xxx" By citing the real name of the person who you got the quote or concept from allows you to quote others without risk of liability. This is a way to break up your talk at that moment, or you can have the audience guess who the person you were quoting is, or was.

Getting your audience involved or into a state of wonder just to bring them back to center as you go on with your talk is always a great thing. This is not something that I would recommend doing often, but I have seen it used and even with the owner of the quote or concept being in the room. It is sometimes used then as a way of giving respect in a playful way to your co-host and getting a chuckle out of them and out of the audience. Humor at the right time works well to boost your "Powerful Public Speaker" Index (PPSI).

Use this Powerful P with caution, but if you use it, you might as well have fun with it.

Pile

How many pieces of wood are too many? It depends on the purpose of the wood. If it is needed to build a fire, you may need a different amount than if you are building a hut or a different type of building structure.

How many snowflakes are too many? It depends if we need the snowflakes to make a ski slope. Skiing is no fun if there are patches of grass sticking through the snow, it must be well packed.

How many stories are too many in a talk? The answer is the same, it depends.

This is a powerful tool if used in moderation and not in excess. Pile means a heap of something. To be a powerful public speaker you DO want to pile on impact. You want the audience to be so full of impact that they say to themselves or out loud that "this was definitely a worthwhile use of my time."

That is it.

The not so impactful use of pile is if you pile on the stories, statistics, the references, the pauses often. Anything done in excess in a talk is not good. Too many jokes, too many opinions vs impactful wisdom, too many stories. After all, have you ever heard a speaker and said to yourself or said out loud, "Ughhh, not another long-drawn-out story?"

Please do not be the center of this type of pile. Keep your talk focused on what is impactful and do not go overboard in areas that do not matter and that do not add value. Of course, when you are in the midst of the talk, something might remind you of a story, and then that story reminds you of another story, and before you know it you are down the rabbit hole of stories and not on the path of the intent of your talk at all.

The same goes for humor and statistical references and many other areas. You may have good intentions, but your mouth needs to only say the things that are needed for impact.

Depending on the audience, this "pile" can turn into a thumbs down for you and not boost your PPSI at all; it may even detract from it.

There are fixes for this: making an outline, determining how much time you have, and sticking to the plan. Anything not on your plan must pass the "does this deviation truly add value, impact, and substance to my talk or not?" If this is not answered as a definitively 100% truth, then don't deviate.

Remember, when you are using a negative pile to show your journey to the depths of a downfall, layering them for great impact, bringing the audience back to the top with your positive piling and layering can be a really effective and powerful tool to empower them.

Polish

A vase is beautiful. After years of use, it may need to be polished.

Once polished, it is beautiful again. The owner must work at keeping it looking nice by polishing it from time to time. Let us now relate this to public speaking.

This word is different than the word perfect. What is meant by polish is that you do the best to practice your public speaking to smooth out the rough edges. So, what is a rough edge in public speaking, you might ask? Good question.

Below, I want to share a list of things that could be considered rough edges. I've heard some of these time and time again in conferences. I have also heard some points talked about in different ways by the many powerful public speakers that are in my circle.

Remember, smoothing out the rough edges in your talk is not the same as perfection. There's a section related to being perfect that is also in this book. Take a look at that as well.

Now, let's look at our list related to rough edges:
- Saying 'Ummm'
- Having awkwardly long pauses
- Forgetting what comes next in your talk
- Smacking your lips
- Having to read off of your paper
- Not knowing what to do with your hands

- Skipping around on your points and not following your outline
- Not speaking clearly
- Crying uncontrollably during your talk
- Not having a clear transition between the sections of your talk
- Inaccurate references
- Adding too much to your talk, causing it to be too long
- Not speaking loud enough
- Taking out too much from your talk, causing it to be too short
- Trying to be funny when it's inappropriate
- Having awkwardly long eye contact with one member of the audience
- Pacing too much on stage

Review this list above. Smooth the rough edges. Mark where you are now. Emotions may come up and come out. Be prepared for this possibility. When you voice something, it may cause emotions. That is ok. How you handle it is what matters. When we are in front of an audience, your poise is not exactly what matters, but your impact.

Check your progress every several weeks as an example.

See the progress to powerful.

Keep doing this and looking back to see where you have come from.

Feel the power.

Feel the impact.

Gain the strength.

Now monetize it.

- Step 1: Get a video camera or phone.
- Step 2: Pick a topic.
- Step 3: Pick three speaking challenges to work on.
- Step 4: Turn on the camera and film your practice.
- Step 5: Review your practice and critique it — Score yourself 10 amazing or 1 you need to keep practicing and raising your score.
- Step 6: Repeat.
- Step 7: Perfect your craft as the world's next most powerful public speaker.

You can grab the full and complete workbook to accompany this book by visiting
https://krystyllerichardson.com/51Psworkbook

NOTES and MAKE UP YOUR OWN MIND

ACTION PLAN

Issue: _____
_____
_____
_____

Why should I work on this? _____
_____
_____
_____

What is my desired outcome? _____
_____
_____
_____

Steps to work on this – list top 3 to 5 steps: _____
_____
_____
_____
_____
_____

This must be done by (timeframe/date): _____

_____

_____

If this does not happen, what is the negative effect: _____

_____

_____

_____

_____

I proclaim that I will: _____

_____

_____

_____

_____

_____

_____

_____

_____

_____

_____

Powerful Practice Groupings

Stop where you are in this book. Time to practice.
Pick 3 of the Powerful Public Speaking Ps
Write what it is about these 3 that you want to perfect
Practice 7 times over a set period of time
Each time, take notes and adjust as needed
Determine your score or have others determine a score
Are you getting better each time?

Powerful Public Speaking P Date: Practice # :	Score (1-10)
1.	
2.	
3.	

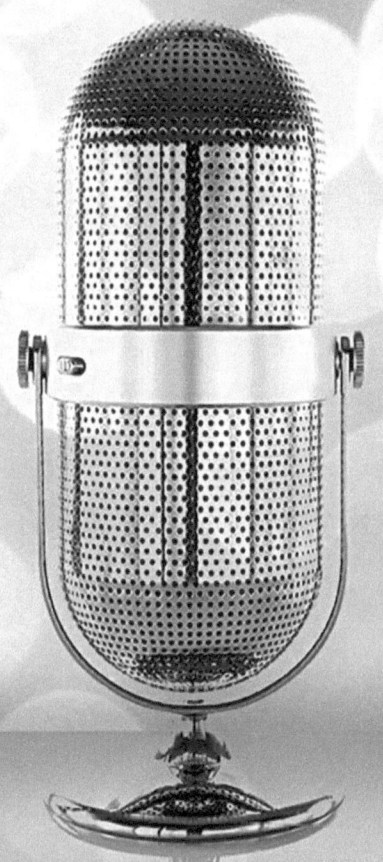

"Time for lift off. Time for impact. You must first be transformed by your words before you can transform others."

Krystylle Richardson

28

Primetime Prep

Talk to yourself.
Encourage yourself. Make the best out of the speaker self-talk pep talk.

Prime time is fast approaching. You are bubbling with excitement. You may be bubbling with fear. You may be bubbling in your rear. Yes, it's true. Many times, when people are excited or nervous, they end up having to go poop before they speak. Is that you? Not every time but some of the time, that is me. In this section, we are going to look at self-talk and not necessarily our bathroom habits. I hope it made you smile, or you may be disgusted. Either one is fine.

Some of us may be fortunate enough to have a whole cheering squad and pep talk squad following us everywhere we go to speak. The rest of us have to talk to ourselves. You may be going over your talk in your mind. You may also be going over various emotions related to either the excitement or the fear connected with the talk you are about to give. For some, it does not matter if it's a large audience or a small audience. They are just downright afraid. I have a definition for fear that we will be going over in one moment. What I want to talk about first, though, is the pep talk.

Positive affirmations do work. Do you have a list of affirmations that you use daily? Do you have a list of affirmations that you use specifically if you're about to go and give a talk? Public speaking can be intimidating to some. It's not that it even has to be intimidating, it's just that you want to make sure that you give your best because you're so excited about the topic. The affirmations that I'm speaking of are ones that you should be using before the date of the speaking engagement. Then maybe there's some that you can add on the day of the engagement.

Here are some examples of some affirmations that could help you with positive self-talk. Personal pep talks do work.

- I am a good speaker
- I am confident
- I am a great speaker
- I am a fantastic speaker
- I'm going to go out there and crush it
- I'm going to make sure that I breathe
- I'm going to stand in the way that I do not lock my knees and have the potential to pass out
- I am a go-getter
- I am ready to do this
- I deserve this opportunity, and I'm going to take it
- I'm going to give my all
- I'm going to leave my heart out on the stage
- I am an impactful speaker
- I speak with authority
- I am an expert in my field
- I will not let anything stop me from getting this message out
- I will have fun while I'm speaking
- I will make a point to engage the audience
- I love speaking, and it loves me
- I will not let fear overtake me
- I will walk out there with confidence
- I will smile, and I will enjoy it
- I will share my authenticity with the audience
- If something does not go as planned, it is okay; I can overcome it

- I am a conqueror, and I am flexible
- I will stay aware of the time
- I'll be a good steward of the time
- I will save time to ensure that my concluding thoughts are clear
- I will save time to make sure that I can present my offer and not rush it
- I will not beat myself up if something was not said that was planned
- I will accept the fact that everything that I said was what needed to be said for that audience for the time that we shared
- I will make sure that I provide my contact information so people can connect
- I will ensure that I save time in my schedule to talk to the audience after my speech
- I will not rush off, and I will ensure that I am available for chats, pictures, and whatever the audience needs for a reasonable amount of time
- I will use anything that did not go my way as a lesson learned and celebrate my accomplishments
- I will always keep a positive attitude
- I am resilient
- I am powerful
- I'm a powerful public speaker
- I am me

Did any of these resonate with you? Can you see yourself saying some of these? Have you said some of these? Feel free to use a highlighter to mark where you feel you are now, and then date the color. Then when you come to this section again in the future, use a different color and date the new one. See your progress brighten the way each time!

Make a list and use some of these or make a list of your own. The point is that affirmations do make a difference. Whether you say these in your mind or say them out loud as I do, just say them. Or whether you scream them in the comfort of your car or an empty restroom, affirmation works. You may say some of these, you may not say any of them. You choose, but whatever you do, say something to yourself.

You need yourself. You need your confidence. People can speak over you all they want, but you need to know that you believe in YOU. Say it over and over until you believe it before the day of your talk, also on the day of your talk, and right before it's time for you to go on for primetime.

I also say a prayer and may ask others to pray for me or with me as well. Do whatever you need to do to ensure that you do go out there and crush it. Do whatever you need to do to ensure that people see and hear that you are a powerful public speaker. It's game time. It is time to go out and crush it.

So, let's go!

Primetime Opener

This is an interesting quote:

> *The Public is merely a multiplied "me."*
> *Mark Twain*

For your opener then, do you treat your audience, your congregation, your business partner as a person or set of people who are just like you? This may not be the intent of this quote, but that interpretation serves the purpose of this section. We know that we are all made different. We know that in any group that we speak to, there may be introverts, extroverts, academics, millennials, senior citizens, those that do not have English as their first language, those who are hard of hearing, those with preconceived ideas of whether they are going to listen to you or not, get something out of your talk or not, and those who are just happy and eager to listen and learn from anything and everything that comes out of your mouth. We have mentioned the fact that it is important to know your audience. This is the case related to this quote from Mark Twain. We should not assume that everyone is like us. Powerful public speakers prepare by researching to know as much about their audience as possible. This helps us to know how to start or open our talk, speech, sermon, or meeting.

Over the years, there are various ways that I've seen people open up their talk. Before we get into the list of ways people can start their talk, I want to talk about introductions. It is always good to know who is going to introduce you and give them your bio. This should not be the long version; it should be a very concise version so that the audience does not feel like they're listening to a whole book being read aloud. Sometimes people have a video that introduces them. The same holds for the video. I would recommend only having the intro video be thirty seconds and at the most ninety seconds. People should not feel like they're watching a complete feature film just for your introduction. Remember, we're talking about powerful public speaking. Let the audience hear you for themselves as opposed to having a long intro video to watch. If you have a video, it is good to have clips of other speaking engagements, interaction with the audience, and other things that build anticipation. You want the audience to want to hear you after the introduction, not be turned off by it.

Let's go back for a moment to the person that might be reading your introduction. My name is spelled very uniquely. So, in my introduction, I either have already talked to the person, so they know how to pronounce my name, or another thing I could do is spell it the way that is easiest for the reader. This does not guarantee that the person will not have issues with the pronunciation of other words in the bio, but at least they can make sure that they say your name correctly. Keeping your bio simple with fifth-grade language is always a good rule. Although you may be able to make a comeback and should be able to with your actual speech, you don't want to start with it being opened with low energy or even no energy. During this book, I talked about the fact that sometimes people have a team travel with them. If you can have someone read your bios that you know, such as a person on your team or someone who is used to doing it, that is the best bet. Next, we will discuss how people start their big moments.

Here are some ways that people open up their talk. Think about if you've done these or if you've heard people do any of these:

- Start by saying hello, your name, and gratitude for being there.
- Have someone introducing you.
- Start with a joke, a story, even talking about the weather.
- Start with a welcome, asking "What's up xxx?" (Filling in the city name)
- Start with silence, a sigh, even with a wave.
- Start at the front of the room, from the stage, or from the back of the room or balcony.
- Have music playing, hyped music and a dance before you start.
- Start with statistics, maybe even a question: "Did you know…?"
- Beginning with concluding points or telling them what you're going to talk about.
- Start with a round of applause for the person who introduced you or asking for a volunteer.
- Addressing a technical issue with gratitude for the team who helped you solve it.
- And start with a big, huge smile and eye-to-eye contact

No matter what method you use, make sure that you have some way of capturing the attention of your audience in the first few seconds. This is such a crucial time frame. Five seconds sounds short, but it's long. It is long in the sense that it is long enough for the audience to determine they like you or not. It might even stem over into the trust factor depending on what you say. They may or may not already know you, so you need to think about the know, like, trust factor. If within the first 5 seconds you have offended people already, they will tune out and either walk out or just not pay attention to the rest of what you're saying.

30 and 31

Primetime Storytelling and Pirates

Yet again, I open the topic with a quote that fits perfectly to me:

> *As it is the characteristic of great wits to say much in few words, so small wits seem to have the gift of speaking much and saying nothing.*
>
> *François de La Rochefoucauld*

I love that quote, which takes me to the topic at hand and my word of focus. Relevant.

That is the keyword for this portion of the book. Remember, your public speaking is for the audience. Is this not a time for you to reminisce on stage necessarily? A story must be relevant.

There's a section in this book where I talk about the hero's journey. That is a very good format to use as far as your storytelling is concerned. I've been to many events where someone is speaking. There are conversations after the speech where people are unclear about what certain stories had to do with the subject.

After your speech, you want people to talk about how great it was and how it called them to action. Many of the people in my circle are very good at this. Some people do get off of the point, and then they admit it by saying "I digress." The main advice that I can give in this section is to remain aware of where you are in your talk. That might sound like it goes without saying, but it's true. It's easy sometimes to lose track if you're not clear about your outline.

Many of us have been present when the speaker has said, "Now where was I?" Sometimes they know where they were and their talk, sometimes they're asking the audience where they were. Sometimes people will remember the stories and not necessarily remember the main title of your talk. The stories have a way of making you feel like you connect with the speaker.

My husband, years ago, did a talk about Gorilla Glue. There are still people to this day that bring up that analogy. One guy saw him in the store and said, aren't you the guy that gave the talk about Gorilla Glue? In your stories, having something uncommon with a great meaning is priceless. Tell me, who goes around talking about Gorilla Glue? The way he opened up with the story, gave the analogy, gave information about his issue, talked about how he analyzed what to do, and then how he came out victorious was amazing. I was glad to call him my husband on that day. He got a standing ovation. People came up to him afterward saying that he killed them with that Gorilla Glue analogy. They said that in a good way. I hope that was obvious, but just in case it was not, I wanted to clarify. I smile every time I think about that talk. With me explaining this now, does it make you want to hear the Gorilla Glue story possibly? Maybe we can have the full story published in one of my next books.

Primetime Points

Let's take a look at this quote:

> *What kills a skunk is the publicity it gives itself.*
> *Abraham Lincoln*

Going on and on about yourself during a talk, a sermon, a large or small public speaking event, can be a downer. Here is a short list of things to use your time on during public speaking. Out of the thousands of talks I have heard in my lifetime and specifically now in the personal development space, these key points hold true:

Do	**Do Not**
Do use the time for positive impact.	Do not use the time to solely focus on updates regarding your personal life.
Do use your personal life stories where they fit and don't force it.	Do not continue to go down a rabbit hole that you can clearly see the audience is not engaged in.
Do give it your all.	Do not leave any portion of your time unused. Fill the timeslot.
Do consider how people will use the information that you convey.	Do not speak without considering the positive and or negative effect it could have on the listener.

Do	Do Not
Do smile and frown and convey your passion for what you are saying so others can feel it too.	Do not worry about the faces of those who may be listening. Sometimes they are into you and other times they may be tuned out and thinking about their grocery list.
Do your best to keep your audience engaged.	Do not over try, it turns people off when they sense that.
Do whatever it takes to be the best YOU that you can be.	Do not be so worried about the audience that you miss ensuring that you remain true to your main points.

There is certainly more that could be added to this list. I want to keep us focused. After all, prime time is what we have been working towards, right? You have prepared, you have checked off all of the boxes regarding what is most important for you to say, and you are now saying it.

During prime time, cereal, politics, religion, family planning aka sex, may not be as off limits as it once was; however, knowing your audience can keep you on the road to powerful. Cereal? This is hilarious. The point is, understanding your audience helps to you know if there are some things that might be more controversial than the room can handle, or if everything is fair game to discuss or speak on. Some boundaries are good, others, well, simply make you a dull speaker.

Figure out the best approach based on the audience, figure out what will make you a "stand-out speaker."

Then go for it.

33

Pure

Her facial expressions were an open book of her thoughts.
Her words were placed with care.
Her hand movements were used at the exact right time.
Her heart could be felt and seen with every word she spoke.
Her delivery was pure.

Authenticity is what you can feel, smell, taste a lot of times within the first five to ten seconds of any form of communication. I even love how the word authenticity sounds when it is spoken. It would be hoped that anyone who says anything to a person one-on-one or even in a group, that the person would be true, pure, authentic.

Sometimes the problem is that we are so energized to impress people that we forget our honor. Another thought is that we don't necessarily forget. It's just that we want to impress, so we go for it even if what we're saying is not completely pure. Sometimes immediately, or as time goes by, people will see and feel that maybe we're not speaking from the heart after all.

There was a singer once, who came to the mic and said that they apologized for the condition of their throat and were going to try to do the best they could. As soon as the music started, every note that came forth was in the right key, in the right pitch, and said with power and strength.

So, the statement at the beginning of the song before the music started was questioned by some people as to whether there was an issue with their throat in the first place.

Or did they just say that to gain some compassion for some reason?

Some people were overtaken by the power in their voice and still stand up and clapped at the end. People generally do not want to doubt you or sit with skepticism like those who now questioned the statement given before the song started.

When you're doing public speaking, always be mindful of what you're saying to the audience from a prelude perspective and in the middle of a speech and with your ending. Going back to the singing example, I might stand up and give an ovation myself if a person did not necessarily hit every note correctly, but you could feel their heart based on the words and their expression and the story that they told based on the song.

A speaker who always got nervous every time she spoke would mention it at the beginning while her voice was still shaking. She continues to speak and push through the nervousness and eventually can calmly continue on with her talk in a very inspiring and motivational way. Now of course, this could have been fake, but how she talked about her life and the obstacle she had to overcome to be on stage at that particular time felt like they rang true. It also felt like she was really sincere about her nervous condition. To this day, I still admire her and appreciate her sharing that with us and how she motivated me to continue even if I have a butterfly or two myself.

Often people hear that as soon as someone asks a question, someone else had that same question. The same is true when someone says that they've been through something. There's likely someone else who has been through a similar situation and feels stronger because of someone being vulnerable enough to share.

Be genuine, be authentic, be pure. I would enjoy the purity of a talk over one with flowery words.

34

Passion

You made me feel like I was actually there.

I could visualize your circumstance you described, based on your energy and passion.

Have you ever heard those words after a talk you did?

Do you have passion?

Read this quote:

> **We must distinguish between speaking to deceive and being silent to be reserved.**
>
> **Voltaire**

What do you stand for?

I cannot stress enough how important it is to have passion in everything that you're saying in any type of public speaking. As I've mentioned before, the number of people you're speaking to does not matter. If you're speaking with one person, fifty, two hundred, or five thousand, passion is a must. People want to know that you believe what you're saying and that you have fire in your soul for what you're saying. Napoleon Hill talks a lot about burning desire. This was true in 1938 and is still true today. You have to have a burning desire related to your talk. If people don't feel the energy, then why should they listen.

It's not just a feeling; it's also what they see. Do you know that you can see fire and passion? Well, you can. Hopefully, you can even feel

Passion

it coming off of these pages. This is one thing that is very, extremely important to me that we all get. Again, I know I say that about a lot of the points, but it's true. Passion is king.

Have you ever seen or heard of a public speaker that did not have great content but had passion? You may have also seen people then going to the back of the room to purchase whatever the speaker had on sale only because of the speaker's passion being so high that people felt they needed to get the next thing on offer. Public speaking does not always have to do with purchasing anything; it also has to do with impact.

I talk a lot about impact. Passion is key for that as well. Other people will want to join you, and we will be talking about the partnership in one of the other sections of this book. If you have passion, even if people don't exactly know what they will do to help, they will want to join in partnership with you simply because of your passion. Yes, the message behind what you're doing, the purpose for what you're doing, all of that is important. But I'm telling you, passion is king.

Now it is not good to build a public speaking business on passion alone. People do need to see, hear, taste, and feel that you have that confidence about what you're saying.

You see this time and time again on game shows. A person has to answer, and the other person has to guess whether that person's answer was right or wrong; if they agree with them, and the answer was right, they win money. If they agree with them and the answer was wrong, they don't get the money. So that person giving that first answer sometimes is so passionate and sounds so confident that the person agrees with them, and it ends up being wrong. Why is that? It's because they had that burning fire that made them appear like what they're saying was true.

This brings me to my next point. Do not use your passion to convey something that's not true. Your passion should be around facts. Your passion should be around something that happened to you that you can convey so that someone else is impacted positively by your talk. In the game show example, it shows that someone can use it just to get their point across but not for the intention of goodness. It's almost always for ego.

So, let's go build good passion skills. We will be talking about your pitch and inflection in your voice and modulation so that people can even hear your passion.

People will grade or rate your passion. There have been many speaking engagements where I get comments either during the engagement with online comments or after the speech if it's in person. People come up to me and say, "Your talk was on fire!", "Oh my gosh, I could just feel your energy!". They will also say "You just drew me in from your first words because of your fire and your passion. I want to work with you. I know that you are the person that I'm supposed to be working with because you will drive me, and I want to have that same fire and passion that you have."

Has anyone ever said that to you about anything in your life? If not, chances are you're not giving your best, and you're not giving your all. You're not doing the things that you can do to have people see and feel your passion. A lot of times when I'm writing books, I don't say the word you in sentences. In this case, I am sharing this with you because I want you to feel that you are reading this book for a purpose, you know that you have more to offer.

You know that if you apply what I'm saying in this book, you too can be a powerful public speaker. You too can show the world that you have passion. If I were to have you stand up in front of a room right now and give even a sixty-second talk about something you know a lot about, could you present your fire in sixty seconds? Would it show up as authentic? Would it show up with true pure flaming fire? If not, you need to keep reading this book, and you also need to contact me related to coaching on powerful public speaking.

With this, you have to be willing to work, and you have to be willing to pull from the depth of your soul to give every single talk all the passion you possess. The passion that you have for your particular topic has to shine through and come through and burn with flames hot every time.

So, I ask you?

Are you up for that challenge?

Passion.

This powerful key is so important.

Do YOU have it?

35

Poking

A little bit here.
A little bit there.
Not too much here.
Not too much there.
How much is too much? Let's explore.

This can sometimes be a sensitive area. I have seen and heard speakers that have done a great job of building in humor in their talks. Others, not so much. Some have poked fun at themselves, and it went really well. Others, it has just seemed downright awkward. The same for poking fun at others in the audience or others that are not even there. This can be touchy.

Stand-up comedy is a form of public speaking. Poke is sometimes used by the comedian to turn the attention back to the audience. I mentioned that this can be too touchy a situation up above, and it is true in this case as well. Not everyone has the same sense of humor, so be careful. During the times that it is done carefully, it is like watching a seasoned surgeon perform an operation. As the jokes skillfully roll off the tongue of the comedian, the audience is eating it up, enjoying themselves, and are not feeling like it is a rude poke at all.

Unless you know the people personally and have a way that you have perfected doing this, it is usually not a good idea to make fun of the audience or point out a flaw in their outfit or hair or anything for that matter.

This is not something that brings power to your public speaking but is a way to ensure that you will not be asked to come back (if you make it out without being confronted).

Powerful public speakers ensure impact without making anyone feel less than or inferior.

Avoid this at all costs.

36

Penetrate

Wow that made me think.

Your talk was brilliant, I never thought of that until you brought it to my attention.

A day has not gone by that I have not thought about the words you spoke that day.

I immediately took action based on your talk.

Have you ever heard phrases such as these after a talk you delivered?

This is called impact. Impact in this form, we will change to a word that starts with P and call if penetration.

There are numerous words to describe how important it is to not just talk but to talk with the purpose of changing a situation, changing someone's life, changing or transforming the mindset of the hearer.

Your ability to have an impact sometimes might come from the method of your talk.

Here are some of the methods:

- Written or manuscript - word for word
- Impromptu or topical - real-time authenticity
- Conversational - comfort and connection
- From memory - demonstrate expertise in the area being orated

Let's also look at some methods that can also be used inside of any of the above methods.

- Timebound talks - The main focus is to stay within a time frame, for instance, ten minutes or two minutes

- Talks with props - The main focus is to have visuals for the audience
- Talks per a teleprompter - The focus is to ensure everything that was planned was said
- Use of metaphors - The main focus is to make as many parallels as possible so that the listeners have a vivid visual
- Use of high fives - The main purpose is to have engagement in connection with the audience
- Use of hands up - Here, the purpose is to engage by people taking sides or voting
- Use of standing clap - The purpose here could be to show complete buy-in from the audience
- Use of a standing survey - Standing to say that you agree with something when you vote as even more of a commitment than holding up your hand. The purpose here may be to request or poll your complete commitment to one of you versus another

With all of the things that have been outlined in this book, it is important that you start strong and end strong.

Everything in between is important, yes, but people will definitely be remembering your beginning. They will also remember your end.

So, make sure that you have something to say that has impact and power, at least at the beginning and the end.

Paint and Connect

I find this to be true:

If you make yourself understood, you're always speaking well.

Molière

Painting was always fun as a child. I would help paint inside the house, changing one room color to another color. Taping off the baseboards and making sure that the line was perfect once the tape was removed. I also used to help my dad paint outside as well. Again, there was a lot of taping. But the end product was a beautiful home with beautiful colors. It didn't matter that we were in a not-so-good neighborhood in Flint, Michigan. Our house was one of the best, if not the best-looking houses on the block because we always had a well-manicured lawn, fresh paint on the house every few years, and lots of love.

Public speaking is a way for you to paint as well. It is a way for you to connect with the audience based on your story. The one that I just told related to actually painting with my dad may have sparked a memory for you. It may also have warmed your heart to think about a little girl that enjoyed spending that type of time with her father. It may have also given you a mental picture of a nice home that was full of love. Looking at public speaking this way shows that it is an art form.

Some storytellers are very, very good. You feel like you can feel the sunshine on your face, smell the soup that was in the pot, hear the birds chirping, and the list goes on and on. They make their story so vivid that you feel like you're actually there. Sometimes you feel like you're actually the character that they have described.

This brings me to the hero's journey. Some of you may have heard of it. Being able to tell a story in a way that brings excitement shows that the person has gone through some kind of struggle, they go through a defeat, they find someone that can potentially help them, they may accept or reject their advice, they have to climb from the bottom to the top of their situation, their mental and physical fortitude draws you in, they celebrate at the end because they had challenges and were able to conquer them to receive the victory. How delightful it is to be able to give someone a mental picture of all of that and maybe a two to five minute or even ten minute story. You don't want to spend too long on it but just enough to be able to give the audience a feel for the journey.

Being able to do this time and time again using various stories in your life takes practice. Once you've mastered the ability to paint a picture for people, you are well on your way to being the world's next powerful public speaker.

I want to challenge you right now to pick three stories in your life where you've had some challenges, but you've come out on top.

Write down maybe five to seven points about that story using the hero's journey model. You can feel free to look on the internet for the specifics of that model because I will not list them here.

What I want you to do is write those points and think about how you felt when you were going through it.

Write down words like sad, happy, excited, fearful, undecided, honored, skeptical, and so on.

Writing down the feelings associated with the various parts of the story will help you better outline how you're going to tell the story and make sure that you incorporate words, gestures, voice tones, voice patterns, and facial expressions that express those words.

All of these things help you to paint the picture and to draw the audience in and therefore help you to be more impactful as a speaker. They will connect with you because they might say to themselves, "Wow, I felt like that before." They may feel like they have been in your shoes, sometimes they will have compassion or empathy based on what you're going through, but it's because they feel it.

Before you start writing, I invite you to reflect back on when you've said something to someone or attended a speaking engagement where someone uses the word feel. Someone came up to you and said that you made them feel a certain way based on what you said.

The next question is, was that the feeling that you were going for? You might need to evaluate how you want it to convey those emotions. One of the main points here is that even if you run a race that you did not win, you always find a way to choose your words so that you come out on top. Winning the race is not the point. Having a lesson learned that made you a better person is the point. This shows that you came out on top as a person who now has a better understanding of that particular situation.

With all of this writing you are doing specifically for your hero's journey, remember to write your entire talk, rewrite it, and write it again. Why, you may ask? This helps you to refine it a bit each time, and it gives you the practice you need to get closer and closer to your own talk. This helps you to be able to shift if needed due to the audience's engagement or interest in what you are saying. The hero's journey can be a fun experience for the audience if used effectively. It can draw them in, inspire, engage, create wonder and various emotions and have them wanting more.

Life Story Challenge – Try your hand at writing an engaging and inspiring life story.

_____
_____
_____
_____
_____
_____
_____
_____
_____
_____
_____
_____
_____
_____
_____
_____
_____
_____
_____
_____

> You can grab the full and complete workbook to accompany this book by visiting
> **https://krystyllerichardson.com/51Psworkbook**

Here is an interesting quote related to this topic:

> *There is no private life which has not been determined by a wider public life.*
>
> *George Eliot*

I try to live a life that focuses on lessons learned every day. It is a part of my growth mindset strategy. It has served me well. It is my home; by reading this book, you can strengthen your mindset skills related to not just focusing on winning but focusing on what you've learned and how you can become a person of greater impact because of it.

- Step 1: Pick a topic that you can do a speech on in 2 minutes.
- Step 2: Ask two family members and 2 additional people to jump online to hear your talk — or do this in person.
- Step 3: Tell them you need honest feedback.
- Step 4: Do the talk.
- Step 5: Ask for written feedback — short — in general and on specifics you were hoping to perfect.
- Step 6: Thank them.
- Step 7: Review input and make corrections as needed.
- Step 8: Perfect your craft as the world's next most powerful public speaker.

You can grab the full and complete workbook to accompany this book by visiting
https://krystyllerichardson.com/51Psworkbook

Pause

Stop.
Take a breath.
Look at the audience.
Provoke thought.
These are forms and outcomes of the word pause.

This is a very important word; it just is one of a number of the words we have looked at that are very important and powerful.

Take a look out at the audience, what is going on? Are the people resonating with you? Are they engaged? Are people talking with each other, making notes?

Are there people getting up and walking out, which can be very disheartening, especially if you've taken a lot of time to prepare or even taking time to drive or fly to wherever the engagement is.

Another thing that may be disheartening is if you have an emotional bond to what you're saying, and people seem to just not be getting it

But it may not even be related to what you're saying but to the way that you're saying it. This means your delivery. This book will get into hand gestures, facial expressions, the way you stand, the inflection in your voice, etc. It is important to never forget who you are speaking to and why.

Go more into detail here about the pause for effect, the pause of connecting with particular audience members, or maybe a pause to take a breath, as a question. These are equally important pauses.

- Step 1: Pick three short talks by your favorite speakers.
- Step 2: Evaluate their use of pause.
- Step 3: Write down what they could do differently.
- Step 4: Film yourself and incorporate the art of pause.
- Step 5: Evaluate and determine what you could do differently.
- Step 6: Perfect your craft as the world's next most powerful public speaker.

You can grab the full and complete workbook to accompany this book by visiting
https://krystellerichardson.com/51Psworkbook

Pissed

That got under my skin.
Oh my, I cannot believe it.
He did what, she said what?
That got me going.
These are all phrases used in this context of being pissed.
What I mean is, what is it that gets you fired up? What is it that gets under your skin? What is it that you see as an injustice in the world?
Here is an interesting quote:

Generally speaking, if a human being never shows anger, then I think something's wrong. He's not right in the brain.

Dalai Lama

For the purposes of this discussion, I will be substituting the word anger with the word emotion and or passion.
One of the main things that I've seen as part of powerful public speaking, specifically when I talk with the people in my circle and beyond, is emotion and or passion. Being able to convey strong emotion in verbal form, eloquently, and with passion is a big plus. Have you ever noticed public speakers who have everyone on the edge of their seat, people on the edge of tears if not completely bawling? People, who at the end of whatever it is that they're saying, then have an immediate standing ovation?

Authentic emotion is power.

Some people try to stay strong and try to hold back tears or from getting too riled up. Those are the very things that connect with the audience. This is also something that must be done with the proper motive, once again meaning authenticity. People can smell a phony a mile away. Sometimes not, though. If you can turn on and off concerning your emotion, it sometimes rubs the audience the wrong way. They then begin not to trust you, maybe not even like you, which is not why we speak. We speak so that people get to know more about us. So that we can authentically check off the boxes of know, like, and trust.

I want to make sure that I covered this section by just giving you an introduction to what I meant by the word pissed. Suppose there's something that's going on in the world that gets under your skin. You may want to incorporate it into a story that you can tell during your talk. Other people may rally around that same thing. There are also people in the audience who may feel opposite to what you feel related to that particular initiative. That's okay. At least it shows that you stand for something.

It can be a turn off in public speaking if a person does not take a stance. They give both sides of the story and never say what they feel. It may be because they don't know, and they're just talking to fill the time. Don't be that person. People will respect you if you stand for something, even if they don't agree with you.

So be raw and real, and please do not show up on stage in the state of being pissed as per the English understanding of the word!

40

Pick

I stand for (you fill in the blank).

My platform of choice today is to focus on (you fill in the blank).

I want to bring your attention to (you fill in the blank).

This is an area of powerful public speaking that is very close to my heart.

We all have something that we stand for. This short section is here just to encourage you to remember your why.

The first question should be, though, is do you have one? Some people have a "Why" which is to do with the fact that they do what they do to provide a better life for their family. Others say they do what they do, public speaking in this case, so they can have impact.

One way to be even more impactful during your talk is to refer to an organization you run, an organization you support or simply want the audience to support. There is nothing that is more impactful than speaking and sharing in a manner that allows the audience to have a tangible impact in the community, country, and world.

Public speaking is a way to use your platform to bring a positive change to those in need. Remember this powerful public speaking position and make a difference every chance you get.

41

Permanent

I will start out this section with a short list of questions for you.

Can you remember a time that you heard a talk, and you could recite almost all of the person's key points?

Can you remember a talk that when it was over someone came up to you to discuss the talk, and you could not remember one point?

Can you remember a talk that someone that was not there asked you what the topic was, and you had to struggle to remember?

Take a moment to think about several examples related to the questions above. This will help you to assess the word permanent.

What can you do, say, or not say during your talk to have an image permanently etched in your audience's mind? Be rememberable for good reasons. Be the outstanding speaker. Be the speaker of impact. Be the one they want to hear over and over. Be the difference maker.

Think about speakers that have points you remember even today from years ago, or even months ago. Think about why. Likely it is the way they made you feel. The point hit home as they say.

Be a hit-home speaker. Study the greats and what points stuck to you.

Make your own power points using their models or one of your own.

When speaking, remember to anchor your points. That can be done by repeating them several times during the talk. Some people also give a summary or a conclusion at the end where they list out various bullet points. Other times people have the audience repeat the points during the talk and at the end. Having a vivid example related to your points can also ensure that the listeners have something that they can connect with related to the points that you want to have extend their minds.

Plenty of people have been victorious using this technique and you can be too. I have had plenty of experiences where I've gotten lost in a story I was telling and could not remember how to tie it back to the point that I was trying to make. The reverse is also true. Being a good storyteller takes practice. Being a good storyteller that has key points that people will remember and not just remember the stories is also something that takes practice. In today's world, there are all types of speaking outlets. Internet news, podcasts, streaming channels, and big stages all have commonalities. We want to have our key take aways permanently etched in the minds of our audience. Using anchor words can do that for you. Using repetition can also help. Having the audience repeat short phrases after you is another great technique. The brain is one complex operating system that prefers to focus on one idea at a time. Be a speaker who can speak five minutes, twenty minutes, or even sixty minutes on a topic as one idea. This gives you and your talk a better chance at being memorable. Giving your audience a reason to care is key and using wording that allows them to give you permission into their minds helps as well. You may then be known as the polite speaker. When you weave what they already know with the new perspective of the concept you have as your one idea, you are winning points as a powerful public speaker. Feel free to pause for a moment and think of one of your life stories. Get us a life lesson from that story. Take time right now to practice this art form. To provide a guideline, maybe you can tell yourself to keep the story to less than five minutes. Time to create permanence. I hope you did well.

# Ponder

This word has an old feel to it for me, I am not sure why. When I think of the word ponder, it takes me to a time in my life when I spent summers with my grandparents. We would sit on the porch for a spell and look over the garden. We might even sit on the driveway and water the garden and "ponder" what would be our next set of chores to do to maintain the garden until time for harvest. That is what I think of when I hear this word. Now let's look at it in the form of public speaking.

Time to focus on what you want the audience to focus on after they are gone.

Give your audience things to ponder.

Sometimes it is public speakers who are so into what they are saying that they forget that the purpose of the talk is to impact the audience. It may be that you want them to think or feel a certain way. It may be that you want them to buy something. It may be that you want them to take action in their own lives or the lives of their family, business, and so on. Having a talk that does not end with some type of call to action is a missed opportunity in my book. This is not to be judgmental at all. But this is to say that you have the undivided attention of a group of people. It could be one person, twenty people or one thousand. The question then is, what are you going to do with this power? What are you going to do to shift someone's mindset or someone's finances? Think about what type of call of action that you can have. Consider a call to action.

Give the audience something to ponder. It is not always about giving the audience an assignment but using that precious time wisely.

So, I ask you, based on this section of the book, what are three things that you might do differently in your next talk because of this section?

Pondering is good. Action is good. Let's think about how we can make an impact and make it.

… 43

Primetime Conclusion

Have you heard a speaker say, and in conclusion?
 Or hear them say, here are some final thoughts?

By now, the audience should be very engaged in what you're saying. You should have them sitting on the edge of their seats. That would be mentally at a minimum, if not even physically. They should be asking themselves, "What are they going to say next?" During many virtual speaking events, the audience sometimes type comments. There may be comments throughout the person's talk. As you approach the end, it should be your hope that people are really feeling it. People are really feeling you. People are engaged to the point that it doesn't matter what your call to action is. They're going to do their best to do it.

I want to talk here about your conclusion. In my opinion, there always should be some type of summary. Leaving your audience hanging with many points that you talked about and not having a way to round up everything for a smooth landing may not be good. I would say always have at least three to five different concluding points. This makes it easy for you to remember and easier for the audience to write down and ponder.

You should remember the word ponder from one of the previous sections. For your concluding point or points, remember your key story, your one key story, and have one point or three at the most for them to remember for your conclusion.

Focus on that one big teaching point that you wanted to get across in your story and present that. Pick something that informs and inspires.

Pick a point that has a wow factor that shows off your authenticity and your boldness at the same time.

Ensure that you understand the culture and other audience dynamics so your final point can fit the situation.

Some people love taking notes, others prefer simply listening and remembering. Be the powerful public speaker that feeds both mind types. Be flexible to follow your instincts based on how the talk is going. If you are getting audience feedback, head nods, claps, and engagement on one area of your talk verses another, think quick on your feet and determine if a revised final main point is better that what you have rehearsed. This shows that you are a masterful and even more powerful public speaker.

Targeting something that you know will benefit the audience verses something that is about you to artificially make you appear more important is key to choosing the right final point as well.

When you focus on one and only one concluding point that is powerful, memorable, and impactful, you have won. You don't want to say your entire talk over again in your conclusion.

So, make it easy and simple to remember for the audience. If the points are too long, they're going to give up writing, or they're going to even just give up thinking about them.

I am in love with acronyms, so I might have the conclusion be an acronym. For instance, if my talk is about power, I may have an abbreviation with a different word for each letter of the word power.

This is a great way to have people remember your final points.

44

Primetime Offer and Final Close

This is an area that has many ways to go about it. Some speakers are so calculated, and others have a minimal approach.

One of my main points of advice is to rehearse your conclusion and close. This is the last thing that the audience will hear and your last opportunity to have major influence on their next thoughts and actions. This holds true for a speech on a big stage, as well as a podcast or internet news report segment.

How many times have you heard a speaker online and LIVE and you were captivated by their every word and then… well… there was no call to action.

A very good call to action is the key. What do you want the people to feel, think, and do at this point? Be clear on it. Be clear on the call to action and be clear about how the audience can get in contact with you. Same thing as above. It is not good to put the task on the audience to hunt and search through the worldwide web to find your name, your website, your email address, your phone number, your social media handles, and… well… you get the point. This is another one of those priceless value-added portions of this book.

Let's go into this a little further from a slightly different perspective.

At the end of some people's talk is when they want to propose to the audience related to something they want them to purchase. For some, this is a very uncomfortable time. For others, they do it so smoothly that the audience doesn't even know they are being sold to. The transition into this time of a talk should be rehearsed over and over again. You don't want to come off as being salesy. A lot of public speakers that have something to sell just state one price, others say "This is the value of the item, but for today I'm offering it at XYZ price."

Which way do you prefer, both as the audience member and as the speaker? Which way would you prefer to make an offer? There are many things to think about here. What I'm doing in this book is sharing with you a number of the options that you have. There are complete books and courses on how to do this with mastery. This small section in my book is to get you to think about what fits best for your purposes and to develop what works best for you.

Let's talk further about the close.

This is also the time for you to give your contact information and to give your final salutations to the audience. Always remember to say thank you to the audience. People have probably paid money to hear you speak, and they have all given their time. I just think it's a polite thing to do to say thank you at the end of your talk. What I've just done in the above paragraph was to give you many ways that you could end your speech. See if you can go back through the section and pick three to five ways that were just given. Did you find all of them? I hope that you did. If not, take a look again.

One of the last things I would like to say is about after the close. It's always good to have a clear statement of where you will be after the talk. Don't have them guess, let them know you will be in the lobby, at your book table, in the back of the conference area. A lovely idea is to say you're going to lunch and people are welcome to join you. There are many ways to handle this. Just make sure you say something.

Again, do not leave your audience hanging, invite them to connect with you as this also helps to show how approachable you are. It lets them know that you are open and available and will still be in their presence even after the talk.

Connection, connection, connection, it matters.

Figure out a way that works best for you based on the venue and based on the type of speaking engagement. Implement one way, and if it works, keep it.

Feel free to change it up here and there.

The main thing is to offer more connection for the audience.

Coming up with a way to do this puts you well on your way to being a powerful public speaker.

- Step 1: Take your mind to the point of your close.
- Step 2: Write out a close for your favorite talk that you currently do or for a new topic.
- Step 3: Determine how you are going to summarize and write a summary; recap your main points.
- Step 4: Now think about your offer for your course or your book or other — write out the offer.
- Step 5: Now determine the words, phrases, stories that will best help you to "fold" in the offer in a way that does not sound "salesy" but rather sincere.
- Step 6: Rewrite whatever part of the conclusion summary, main point recap that is needed to have a good fold in of this offer. Rewrite this portion as many times as needed to have a seamless fold.
- Step 7: Practice this new conclusion and offer ending. Repeat with further rewrites in needed.
- Step 8: Perfect your craft as the world's next most powerful public speaker

You can grab the full and complete workbook to accompany this book by visiting
https://krystyllerichardson.com/51Psworkbook

Protection

This is one of those last but not least type of sections.

Protection is important. During public speaking engagements, you should never divulge information that was said to have been proprietary. This means confidentiality. If you have made a promise or a commitment to someone to never disclose the information, then the stage is not a place for that. Even if you change the names or just say a person said or she said, or he said or try to make it into a parable.

That's just the wrong thing to do. If that happens, then you have now lost all trust from that person.

Integrity is huge in public speaking, again, whether you're speaking to one person or a group.

One thing I know to be true is that you don't want to get a reputation of being a person who cannot hold something in confidence. Most people do not want to hear portions of their life story in your talk. If you know that you want to use something specific to make your point, it might be a good idea to get their permission first. Changing names, places and a few of the facts is a viable option so that no one can figure out who you are referring to, but you don't know who knows who or what so be careful! Get the point across and whilst also keeping the person protected.

There are a few additional points to consider related to protection:
1. Treat others' privacy as you would like to be treated.
2. Be aware of how sharing may make someone feel.

3. Being a good friend is more important than a sharing a good story.
4. Planning your talk helps you to avoid sharing something unscripted.
5. If something does leak out in a talk, be ready to apologize and do what you can to fix the situation.

And remember, not everyone wants their faces or details in your marketing assets, so make sure you obtain permission to use their image or quotes!

NOTES and MAKE UP YOUR OWN MIND

ACTION PLAN

Issue: _____
_____
_____
_____

Why should I work on this? _____
_____
_____
_____

What is my desired outcome? _____
_____
_____
_____

Steps to work on this – list top 3 to 5 steps: _____
_____
_____
_____
_____
_____
_____

This must be done by (timeframe/date): _____

_____

_____

If this does not happen, what is the negative effect: _____

_____

_____

_____

_____

I proclaim that I will: _____

_____

_____

_____

_____

_____

_____

_____

_____

_____

_____

Powerful Practice Groupings

Stop where you are in this book. Time to practice.
Pick 3 of the Powerful Public Speaking Ps
Write what it is about these 3 that you want to perfect
Practice 7 times over a set period of time
Each time, take notes and adjust as needed
Determine your score or have others determine a score
Are you getting better each time?

	Powerful Public Speaking P Date: Practice #:	Score (1-10)
1.		
2.		
3.		

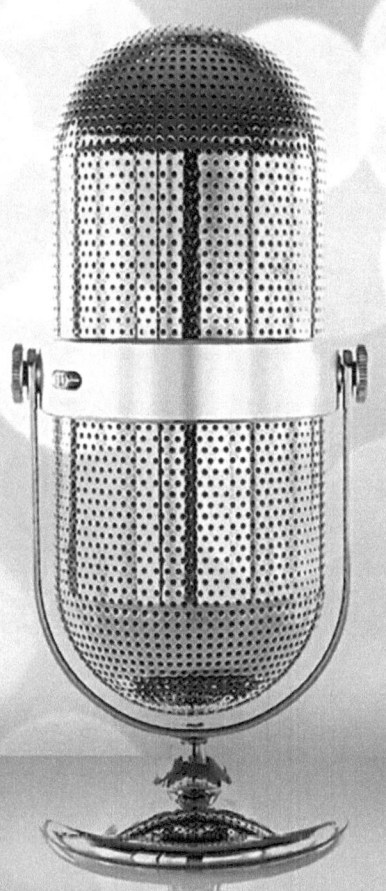

"Happy endings come when you know you have given your all, left it all on the table, went all in, held nothing back, no regrets, no woulda, shoulda, coulda. Happy endings come from knowing that it is really the end that makes way for the newness of the next level's beginnings. Ah, end just in time for the start."

Krystylle Richardson

46

Peace

Peace is an interesting power. It comes in different shapes and sizes for us all. Peace in one person's life might seem like complete chaos to someone else.

When we relate peace to public speaking, it takes on a whole new context.

Here are some points to consider:

1. Peace can come naturally or as something that needs to be nurtured and conquered. Do your best for all of the sections in this book. Make plans to do better the next time. Then, live in peace knowing you did you best.

2. Peace is a good place to be. This is different than being satisfied. Never settle, always be on the continuous improvement path. That is why you are reading this book, right? You know there is more for you in regard to public speaking. Do not sweat the speaking engagements that did not go well. Learn from them and draw on your inner peace to start preparing for the next one.

3. Peace simply means you know that you gave it your all. For that I am proud of you. There is more out there for you though, so don't forget to strive to be higher than complacency.

I remember times in my life when I did not have peace. Sometimes I think about I should have said this, or I should have said that. Overthinking can cause us not to have peace. If you are an overthinker, you understand exactly what I'm saying. As we grow as public speakers, the peace that I speak of here can help you be a better speaker. This means the less stressing that you do about what transpired in the past, the more you can focus on what's next. Utilizing our energy in a positive manner helps us to establish and maintain peace in our lives.

Peace be with you.

Perfect

That was a perfect talk.

Wow, no one could have said that any better.

She was brilliant in her delivery.

These are phrases sometimes said after a person has done a great job to convey a designated message to their audience.

What does this word even mean? Looking at the definition of perfect, it could mean that something is flawless. It could also mean that something is without blemish or defect. It could also mean that something has lined up exactly right. The last one is that everything has gone exactly as planned. It is perfect.

So, I ask you, is that even a real thing? When it comes to public speaking, perfect can take on many different meanings. I think that perfect means you have had an impact on the audience. For someone else, it might mean that they were able to enroll fifty to one hundred people in their new program based on the impact they had from the stage.

For someone else, it could just be that one person's life was saved, and because of your speech, they did not decide to commit suicide. So, I ask you again. What does perfect mean to you? During my masterminds, live videos, public speaking on stage, and other speaking events, I talk a lot about numbers. It may not be in the way that you might think.

Of course, with me, just like within anyone else, if you put a lot of time and effort into something, you want to have the whole world hear what you have to say. You want to have tens of thousands of people listening. That may not always be the case. God might have other plans. It may be that what you have to say was only meant for five people or two people or maybe even one hundred as opposed to the two thousand. With technology today, of course, you can recycle what you've stated, and it can get out to millions of people via YouTube, Roku, and other social media networks. The point here is not to put a lot of unnecessary pressure on yourself. I want to list a few things that will most likely be the case based on your public speaking....

- You may forget some things you wanted to say
- You might look at someone's face, and it throws you off
- You might get encouraged by the crowd and then go off on a tangent
- You might get discouraged by the crowd and feel like you want to end your speech early
- You might have some awkward bodily function happen while you're speaking
- You may have your mind racing in a thousand different directions, which causes you to sound scattered while you're speaking
- You may run out of time, and the conference host tells you it's time to wrap up, and you haven't made it through all of your points
- You may try to make a joke as part of your talk, but no one laughs
- You might get very emotional about something you're saying, and you start crying uncontrollably
- You might say your talk so fast that you're done, and you have not used even half of your time
- You may have an insect that keeps buzzing around your head while you're trying to speak
- You may have a booger right at the edge of your nose that the

Perfect

camera sees, but no one was looking close enough to tell you before the whole thing was filmed

- You may hit a nerve with one of the audience members, and they get up and walk out
- You may have a wardrobe malfunction while you're on stage

And yes … this list could go on and on.

The point of listing these items was not to focus on the negative, but rather to give you pointers on how all of these things can be positive. All of these things could end up increasing your level of impact on the audience. All of these things are real things that have happened during public speaking.

One of the main things I love to tell people concerning public speaking is to own it. If any of the kinds of things happen to you during speaking as are listed above, then own it. This adds to the flavor of your talk. It adds to the reality of our day. Everybody goes through things.

Nobody's life is considered perfect from the standpoint of it has no flaws or no difficulties. What is perfect about it, though, is how we respond. We have an opportunity to have a response or have a reaction. The response should be, in my opinion, that we say, okay, how can I make this situation better, quick, fast, and in a hurry?

My reaction can be frustration and completely falling apart.

My reaction could also be that I roll up my sleeves and do what I have to do to turn the negative into a positive.

I love talking about response and reaction, especially with relation to the word perfect. You see, what makes something perfect is us not internalizing it but rather laughing it off or accepting it as a challenge. Never let something get to you so much that it causes you to have an ulcer or even a heart attack or worse.

Perfect is what we make it. I like that, let me write it again.

Perfect is what we make it.

48

Plenty

There is enough for all.
The possibilities are endless.
No need to fret.

How many people feel that there are not enough speaking engagement opportunities out there? Well, I beg to differ. There are so many different opportunities. The point is to get practice. Have your voice be heard. Make a difference in the world. As you get more exposure, it will get easier. As you get more exposure, it increases your media assets and your social proof. This will lead you closer and closer to being a paid public speaker and not just an oh, you're so amazing, speaker.

I did not want to spend a lot of time in this section but did want to mention that it is important to take advantage of all that the world offers related to public speaking. So don't be afraid, don't be shy, and don't be stubborn. Some people want to get paid right away, and that's fine. More important is the experience in building your credibility. It will be up to you to decide which things that you do for free or less money as opposed to a higher ticket keynote speech.

One way to embody this Powerful P is to prove that you agree with the plenty principle. Here are a few ways to do this:

- Support other people's speaking engagements as a participant in the audience.

- Share speaking engagements coming up, so your speaker friends can speak there as well.
- Share speaking engagements that you are not able to make, but maybe someone else could take advantage of the opportunity.

49

Pudding

Vanilla pudding. Chocolate pudding.
Yum is the word that comes to mind. What about you, do you like pudding?

Simply put, in this section I will say this, be the over achiever. Be the speaker who goes above and beyond even after the talk is over. So many times, we go to an event, we listen to an online summit, and the speakers say their say and say, and, well, then, that's it.

There is no offer to have people contact them, no phone number given for follow-up or questions, no website or social media links, and well, hopefully you get the point. The pudding is power. In this context, it is very important to not let your talk end when the words stop coming out of your mouth. Here are some thoughts:

- Present an ending that sticks with them for hours, days, weeks, and years to come.
- Ensure that the listeners have a way to reach you.
- Give the listeners a prize, free gift, a free session with you, an offer for something that makes them glad that they heard you, and even glad that they stayed until the end of your talk.
- Be unforgettable in a good way by having a unique pudding experience. I would personally love to hear some of your ideas on this myself. Go to my website at krystyllerichardson.com and send a note of some great ways you have found to be unforgettable.

- Last but not least, maybe find a way to be "known" for your pudding. People love feeling personally connected to their favorite speaker. Let's make that you.

50

Please

To please is to satisfy.

To please is to be all for all.

To please is, well, sometimes impossible.

There is a story that shares about a person who was so lonely but yet knew hundreds of people. The person was lonely because they kept allowing themselves to be let down by people who were only in the relationship with them to get what they wanted. They were drawn to this type of person and exhibited the trait of being a people pleaser. The people that they had in their life were self-centered and only wanted their needs met. What a lonely life this person had until they were able to see what was occurring and took steps to rid their circle of such nonsense.

This is also true regarding public speaking. Truth is, there will be people who enjoy your talk, get valid points that they can apply to their lives for years to come. There will also people who will not be pleased, no matter what you say.

You may remind them of a person they had issues with.

You may say something that is a trigger for them in a negative way, and it has nothing to do with you.

You may have a speaking style that is not their preference.

Whatever the case may be, you will absolutely never be able to please everyone. My advice is do not try. Be clear on how you are presenting your points by using some of the powerful techniques and characteristics mentioned in this book.

Do your best to understand your audience type, prepare accordingly, and adjust as needed.

Do all of this knowing that if there is a survey regarding our talk, you might get a person or people who simply are not pleased.

If you know who they are, and feel inclined, you could approach them and ask them their whys and what you could have done differently.

This may be important, depending on if they are mentors, possible business partners, or people who have an opinion you actually care about.

Otherwise, let it go and know that there may always be one.

My last advice in this section is to speak to impact the masses and hope that the rest wake up to your greatness maybe a day or two after your talk sinks in.

We can always hope, right?

Praise

Praise. Lift. Encourage. Give.

Oh, how great it is for someone to GIVE you favorable comments on a talk, on a drawing, on a dish that you cooked, on a thought that you expressed, and the list goes on and on.

Oh, how great it is for you to GIVE a nice comment to someone else who is speaking, to the teacher of your child's band class, to the guard that watches your car for security on a daily basis, for the chef of the restaurant that makes your favor dish and more.

Giving and receiving compliments, nice words, and praise are the little things that someone makes our day. The last Powerful P is one of the most important. It is also true that I may have said this for other sections I know.

There are several aspects to praise. Some may think of this word in relation to church. Others use it as a way to award their team members for a job well done. In public speaking, praise can be a very important final element to help someone know that they are indeed on the right track, they are being impactful, and they are fulfilling a portion of their calling. I truly believe that good, powerful public speaking can be learned, but also has an element of being born with the gift, that edge, the "it." So, the next time you are speaking, do not do it for the praise, but if someone does comment, then, take it all in and use those comments the same way you would other constructive criticism, use it to grow.

Praise

Speaking provides so many learning opportunities. It is my praise for you to say congrats for making it to the end of my list of 51. It is my praise to you for taking the time to do the groupings of the Powerful P's and creating your own exercises to help strengthen yourself in the areas that could use some improvement. It is my praise to you to say you got this, and there is no stopping you now, since you have lots more tools in your toolbox to get you well on your way towards being more powerful than ever on your next stage. It is my praise to you for coming back to this book over and over again, month after month, and even year after year, and thumbing through to find a few hints on areas you could strengthen, and then doing the work to get better. My praise is for you today and always.

We can always improve. I plan to use this book myself to do a few groupings and practice them based on my audience and the purpose of the speaking engagement. I hope you can do the same until you wear out the pages and need to get a new copy, or you bought an extra one to give to a friend to empower them to keep growing. Whatever the scenario, I am proud of you, don't you ever forget it. I would love to hear some of your strengthening outcomes based on using this book. If you send an email to share your strength, to **https://krystllerichardson.com**

I can gift you a chapter from one of my next books for free. So, let's start the exercises, start the shift, and embrace your new power as a public speaker. Until then, remember, speaking is for the hearer more than it is for people to be impressed with you as a speaker, so remember why you are speaking and go rock that stage, that meeting, that one-on-one conversation.

"Speak with power. Live with power. Create a legacy."

Congrats.

- Step 1: Determine why you want to speak on a subject.
- Step 2: Find places that need that subject matter.
- Step 3: Look for places to speak online, at colleges, trade organizations, corporations, industry groups, conferences, summits, and more
- Step 4: Apply to one to five places to speak per week or per month.
- Step 5: Follow up and follow through on checking back with them on your submission.
- Step 6: Review your submission plan and alter it as needed until you start getting booked.
- Step 7: Be ready to discuss your fee, your venue needs, and arrangements.
- Step 8: Perfect your craft as the world's next most powerful public speaker.

You can grab the full and complete workbook to accompany this book by visiting
https://krystyllerichardson.com/51Psworkbook

NOTES and MAKE UP YOUR OWN MIND

Let's think bigger. Pick 10 Powerful Ps to work on rather than the usual 3.

Powerful P - Page #	One Word Description of the Powerful P	Index Rating
1 Page #		
2 Page #		
3 Page #		
4 Page #		
5 Page #		
6 Page #		
7 Page #		
8 Page #		
9 Page #		
10 Page #		
TOTAL	Write total score here	

About Krystylle Richardson

Krystylle Richardson, international public speaker, is the energized creator of Element10™, a creativity to cashflow incubator that helps you do a better job of getting to ten streams of substantial income quicker. She is the ICN Global Ambassador of Innovation, the founder of Life Innovation Global™, wealth advisor, TV show host, pastor, best-selling author, Six Sigma Green Belt, Engineer, and invention/design advisor. Krystylle uses relentless tenacity to move individuals and corporations to sustainable profitability as The JUMPOLOGIST aka The Untapped Income Coach. She is the founder of The JUMP Millionaire Billionaire Alliance where she shares her interviews and personal insights from her network of seven to ten-figure earners built over the past five years.

Krystylle was bullied, which caused her to dig deep to create a higher sense of self-love and purpose. She prayed for God to help her in her search for what she needed and found out others needed the same. She developed a focus on being well rounded related to health, wealth, confidence, spirituality, and understanding the elements needed to build the legacy we all likely desire. Krystylle is a Healthcare Executive by day and a Wealth and Innovation Strategist every other waking hour. As part of the parent entity of Life Innovation Global that teaches in seven areas of life, she also created EMERGE Media Mastery as well as other innovative online courses to help her individual clients and corporations. She has shared with USA Today, Yahoo Finance, NBC, CBS, ABC, Think & Grow Rich Legacy World Tour Producers, Hollywood Glam, Amazon Prime, Thrive Global, Voyage Phoenix, and many other international publications and media outlets, and has been highlighted on e360TV, Voice America, Life Innovation Global TV, and numerous other platforms. Her main focus is pleasing God as a servant leader.

Krystylle has spoken in over thirty-five countries LIVE. She lives out loud and thanks God for allowing her to have an impact while living out her gap and having a blast, teaching others to do the same. Krystylle has been married for thirty years to her wonderful husband and has two beautiful adult daughters. Life Innovation Global™ helps all delegates to be well rounded, just as she has been told that she is. Often referred to as a genius, brilliant, and having a beautiful mind, she is sought out privately by CEOs, doctors as inventors, numerous multi-millionaires and new entrepreneurs for her unique blend of wisdom and ability to provide state-of-the-art practical approaches.

Krystylle Richardson, Global Innovation Leader & Wealth Innovation Strategist, is excited about the virtual induction ceremony with CEO Don Green. She is super thrilled to have the delegation take their places as ambassadors as they learn and execute their lifelong plans to re-imagine their lives aligned with abundance, through innovation, entrepreneurship, and positive change worldwide.

Krystylle's mission is life is simple but vast. Her mission, no legacy unreached, and her life's purpose is to play a part in the lives of at least one billion people to re-imagine and live a life aligned with abundance fueled by innovation and creativity as a limitless lifestyle.

Powerful Practice Groupings

Stop where you are in this book. Time to practice.
Pick 3 of the Powerful Public Speaking Ps
Write what it is about these 3 that you want to perfect
Practice 7 times over a set period of time
Each time, take notes and adjust as needed
Determine your score or have others determine a score
Are you getting better each time?

Powerful Public Speaking P Date: Practice #:	Score (1-10)
1.	
2.	
3.	

Additional Sheets for Future Use

ADDITIONAL SHEETS FOR FUTURE USE

NOTES and MAKE UP YOUR OWN MIND

ACTION PLAN

Issue: _____
_____
_____
_____

Why should I work on this? _____
_____
_____
_____

What is my desired outcome? _____
_____
_____
_____

Steps to work on this – list top 3 to 5 steps: _____
_____
_____
_____
_____
_____

Additional Sheets For Future Use

This must be done by (timeframe/date): _____

_____

_____

If this does not happen, what is the negative effect: _____

_____

_____

_____

_____

I proclaim that I will: _____

_____

_____

_____

_____

_____

_____

_____

_____

_____

Ephesians
Chapter 6, Verses 19 and 20

[19] And for me, that utterance may be given unto me, that I may open my mouth boldly, to make known the mystery of the gospel,

[20] For which I am an ambassador in bonds: that therein I may speak boldly, as I ought to speak.

Amen

About the Publisher

British boutique publishing services are offered by Author Coach, Dawn Bates, an extraordinary woman who specialises in changing the mainstream narratives through the art of literature. Titles published incorporate solo authors as well as a carefully chosen groups of individuals for a wide variety of anthologies in the realms of human rights, social change and cultural diversity.

As well as being an international bestselling author, writer, authority coach, educator and publisher, founder of *Dawn Publishing* Dawn Bates, specialises in developing brand expansion strategies and global visions, underpinned with powerful leadership and profound truths.

She writes for various magazines, and when not travelling or sailing around the world on yachts, she appears on multiple media channels highlighting and discussing essential subjects in today's society.

All the titles published under the *Dawn Publishing* brand bring together the multi-faceted aspects of the world we live in and take you on a rollercoaster ride of emotions while delivering mic dropping inspiration, motivation, and awakening. The books capture life around the world in all its rawness.

Discover more books from *Dawn Publishing* by visiting **www.dawnbates.com/readers**

www.ingramcontent.com/pod-product-compliance
Lightning Source LLC
Chambersburg PA
CBHW030258100526
44590CB00012B/440